D1133976

Basic Box Making

DOUG STOWE

Basic Box Making

The Taunton Press

Text © 2007 by Doug Stowe
Photos © 2007 by The Taunton Press, Inc.
Illustrations © 2007 by The Taunton Press, Inc.
All rights reserved.

The Taunton Press
Inspiration for hands-on living®

The Taunton Press, Inc., 63 South Main Street, PO Box 5506, Newtown, CT 06470-5506
e-mail: tp@taunton.com

Publisher: Jim Childs
Editor: Matthew Teague
Jacket/Cover design: Kimberly Adis
Interior design: Kimberly Adis
Layout: Kimberly Adis
Illustrator: Melanie Powell
Photographer: Doug Stowe

Library of Congress Cataloging-in-Publication Data
Stowe, Doug.
  Basic box making / Doug Stowe.
     p. cm.
  Includes index.
  ISBN-13: 978-1-56158-852-7
  ISBN-10: 1-56158-852-0
 1. Box craft. 2. Box making. 3. Ornamental boxes. I. Title.

TT870.5.S76 2007
684.08--dc22

                              2006022338

Printed in the United States of America
10 9 8 7 6 5 4 3

The following manufacturers/names appearing in *Basic Box Making* are trademarks:
Brusso®, Ives®, Leech® F-26, Liquid Nails®, Masonite®, Ultrasuede®, X-acto®

Working wood is inherently dangerous. Using hand or power tools improperly or ignoring safety practices can lead to permanent injury or even death. Don't try to perform operations you learn about here (or elsewhere) unless you're certain they are safe for you. If something about an operation doesn't feel right, don't do it. Look for another way. We want you to enjoy the craft, so please keep safety foremost in your mind whenever you're in the shop.

ACKNOWLEDGMENTS

BASIC BOX MAKING **IS DEDICATED TO THE STUDENTS** of box making, to whom I pose this challenge: If you want to learn something and get good at it, teach it to another.

I have had many students, both children and adults, who have inspired me to achieve greater clarity of method and purpose. I wish to acknowledge their participation in the making of this book.

Special thanks go to Helen Albert, Julie Hamilton, and Jenny Peters of The Taunton Press for helping this book move smoothly from a concept to a tangible product. I'd also like to thank the designers, copyeditors, illustrators, and experts in photography, printing, layout, and marketing at The Taunton Press, each of whom plays an important role in the success of each book.

Good editors turn woodworkers into writers. A big thank-you goes to my editor, Matthew Teague, for helping to make my words and processes clear and concise.

When I'm finished with a box, particularly one I'm really satisfied with, I leave it on the kitchen counter to receive comments, criticism, and appreciation from my wife and daughter (we all need to show off a bit and share our creations). Thank you Jean and Lucy; you are my best encouragement and support!

Contents

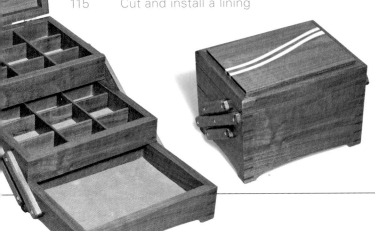

INTRODUCTION

I BEGAN MAKING WOODEN BOXES IN 1976. Aside from the pleasure I found in making them, they served a very practical purpose. Boxes kept me busy between commissions and allowed me to explore designs and techniques without making a large investment in time or materials. Since then I've sold thousands of small boxes through craft fairs and galleries.

I can tell you from personal experience that developing the skills you need to accomplish your best work won't happen overnight. There is a difference between knowledge that you get from a book and skill that takes residence in your own hands. For skill to develop you will need to pay attention, not only to what is told in the pages of a book, but to what the tools tell you: the sight, sound, and feel of their operation, what the wood shares of its own nature, and what your own hands and body tell you of motion and movement.

As your skill develops, you'll begin looking for greater challenges. But don't rush the process. Take your time. Many of the best things that happened in my own work came through repetition of the same simple tasks. Watching carefully, I began to notice things: when cuts could be made more accurately, how processes could be simplified, where finishes could be improved. These things don't come in a rush. Slow down, savor the process, enjoy the special scent of each species, and take time to feel and enjoy the texture of its grain. At the risk of repeating myself, I offer this advice: Repeat yourself. Repetition leads to refinement, and refinement leads to success.

Though it's not necessary to build the projects in this book in any particular order, they are arranged by the level of difficulty. As you grow in confidence working through the projects in this book, use your imagination and ask a few questions: What if this box were made in that wood? What if that joint were used on this box? What if the lid had more overhang? What if I made the box larger, or smaller? The question "What if?" can challenge and engage a box maker for years of adventure. It has for me, and I hope it will for you as well.

A Simple Lift-Lid Box

A BOX, IN ESSENCE, is a very simple thing: a top, a bottom, and four sides. But elevating the form to a higher level of beauty and quality can seem complex. This handsome design is intended as a starting point to teach basic techniques that will lead to better results on more complex projects.

The sides of this box are joined with simple miter joints strengthened by adding keys, a task made easy and accurate using a simple tablesaw jig. A plywood bottom is glued securely into saw kerfs cut in the sides, reinforcing the lower portion of the mitered joints. The lift lid is cut from hardwood and rabbeted for a snug fit.

As a practical matter, this box can be used as a ring box or gift box with this warning: The box may become treasured more than the gift inside. The box pictured here is made of white oak, but by changing the size, proportions, joinery, or wood choices, you can create countless variations on this simple design.

Mitered box with a lift lid

This simple lift-lid design features mitered corners secured and strengthened using keys of a contrasting walnut. The box is made from 3/8-in.-thick white oak and the top is spalted pecan, but either can be made from beautiful scrap lumber you've treasured and saved. Baltic birch plywood is used for the bottom.

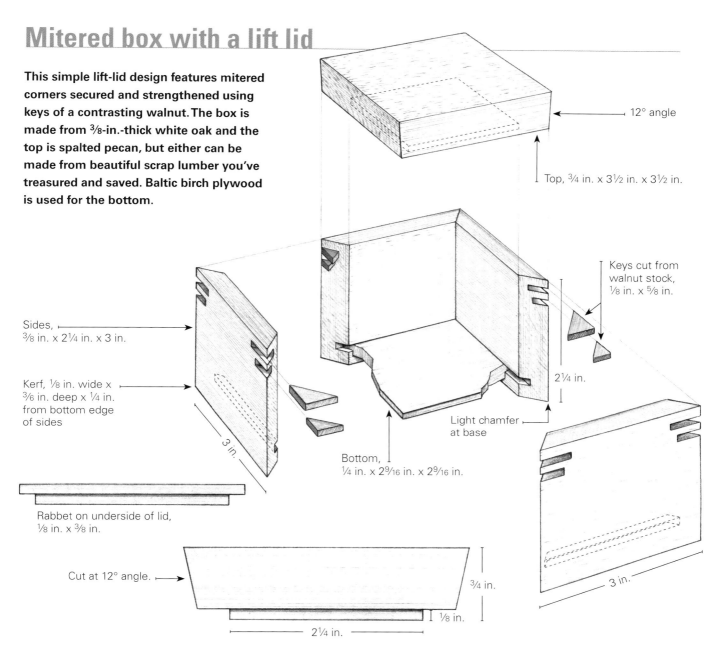

12° angle

Top, 3/4 in. x 3 1/2 in. x 3 1/2 in.

Keys cut from walnut stock, 1/8 in. x 5/8 in.

Sides, 3/8 in. x 2 1/4 in. x 3 in.

Kerf, 1/8 in. wide x 3/16 in. deep x 1/4 in. from bottom edge of sides

2 1/4 in.

3 in.

Light chamfer at base

Bottom, 1/4 in. x 2 9/16 in. x 2 9/16 in.

Rabbet on underside of lid, 1/8 in. x 3/8 in.

3 in.

Cut at 12° angle.

3/4 in.

1/8 in.

2 1/4 in.

MATERIALS

QUANTITY	PART	ACTUAL SIZE	CONSTRUCTION NOTES
4	Sides	3 in. x 2 1/4 in.	3/8-in. white oak
1	Bottom	2 5/8 in. x 2 5/8 in.*	1/4-in. Baltic birch plywood
1	Lid	3 1/2 in. x 3 1/2 in.	3/4-in. hardwood of your choice
16	Keys	1/8-in. thick x 5/8-in. wide	1/8-in. walnut, crosscut at 45° and sized to fit

*Determine actual size by measuring widest point of saw kerf in box sides.

Prepare the stock

THE RIGHT START CAN MAKE OR BREAK
a project: If you don't start with stock that is flat,
square, and straight on all sides, it's difficult to build
a square box. Even a small amount of warp in the
finished stock makes it hard to pull corners together
during assembly, and a poorly fitted joint is doomed
to failure. Fortunately, preparing stock properly is a
simple procedure.

1. Crosscut your stock to a length more easily
handled on the saw. I generally prefer resawing
stock in the range of 24 in. to 36 in.—long enough
to allow a secure grip on the material, but short
enough so it is not hard to manage.

2. Pass either of the rough edges of the stock
across the jointer. You may need to take more than
one pass over the jointer, working until the edge is
flat enough to ride smoothly along the tablesaw's
table in the next step. At this point, however, jointing a perfectly flat edge is unnecessary.

3. Cut the stock to rough width on the tablesaw,
allowing ¼ in. to ⅜ in. more than is required for the
exact dimensions of the box sides. Use a push stick
to finish the cut.

Resawing at the tablesaw

Resawing stock can be done on either the bandsaw
or the tablesaw, but for small stock, as is often used
in box making, the tablesaw is an easier option. I
use a thin-kerf blade because it requires less power
and provides for a slightly greater finished thickness. That said, a standard ⅛-in.-kerf blade will
also work.

WORK SMART

By listening to the jointer's sound as
it works, you can tell if it's removing stock throughout the cut. As the
jointer passes through high and low
points in the edge of the stock, its
sound will vary, becoming more uniform when the stock is straight.

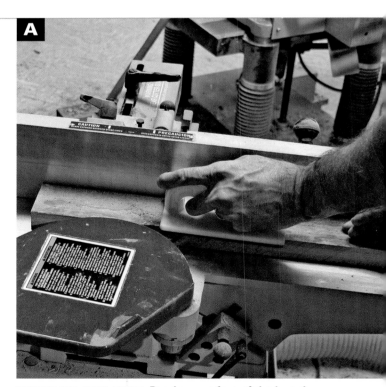

A

SURFACE ONE SIDE Passing one face of the board
across the jointer makes resawing more accurate and safe,
but a perfect finish is not required at this stage. Simply get
one side flat enough to follow the tablesaw fence.

RESAW AT THE TABLESAW Set the blade just over half the width of the stock so that the hands can be kept a safe distance from the blade. Before cutting the second edge, flip the stock end over end, making sure that the same face is against the fence.

WORK SMART

Although it may be harder for the beginning woodworker to imagine the beauty of wood while its grain and color are hidden by a rough surface, the additional thickness of unplaned wood offers greater flexibility for resawing.

1. Begin preparing the stock for resawing by passing one face across the jointer **(PHOTO A)**. At this point, a perfect finish is not required. The stock needs to be flat enough to follow the fence safely. Removing too much stock may limit your options for use of the offcut material or make it too thin for use.

2. For small boxes like this, I often am able to rip right down the middle to get equally thick planed sides, but even thinner stock from offcuts can be useful in other parts of box making. At the tablesaw, don't try to resaw the full height in a single pass.

Instead, adjust the tablesaw's blade height to cut just over half the height of the stock at one time. By reducing the blade height, the stock passes more easily through the cut and there is less risk to the hands. Holding the stock upright and against the fence, take a pass along one edge.

3. Flip the stock end over end, keeping the same face against the fence, and make another cut along the opposite edge **(PHOTO**  **)**.

WORK SMART

Severely warped or twisted stock should be avoided when resawing. Not only will it produce useless material, but cutting it can present a safety hazard, particularly for a less experienced box maker.

Plane and size the stock

A small portable planer is more than sufficient for box making, and it often gives better results than the large planers found in many cabinet shops. Large planers often have serrated infeed rollers that may leave marks when you're removing a thin layer of wood, as is often the case in box making. Small portable planers, on the other hand, enable you to fine tune the thickness by removing small amounts of stock at a time.

1. Your first pass through the thickness planer should be taken with the rough face toward the planer knives **(PHOTO C)**. Plane the material to final thickness by removing small amounts from each side, flipping the stock over between cuts.

2. Once you've reached the desired thickness, smooth one edge of the stock at the jointer **(PHOTO D)**.

3. Cut the stock to finished width by trimming the opposite edge on the tablesaw. Make sure you have a push block at hand to finish the cut. For greater safety, I also use a shopmade zero-clearance insert with an integral splitter, but after-market zero-clearance inserts are available for most saws **(PHOTO E)**.

PLANE DOWN THE STOCK Plane the stock to thickness in small increments, checking the surface after each pass. Defects can often be removed by changing the feed direction of the stock.

JOINT ONE EDGE SMOOTH Use the jointer to square one edge of the stock. Push the stock slowly though the cut and watch carefully for defects that might mar the appearance of the assembled box.

RIP AT THE TABLESAW To cut the stock to width, keep one hand stationary to hold the stock tight against the fence and use the other to feed the stock. Have a push stick ready to finish the cut.

Mark and cut the box sides

WHEN USING OAK OR ANY WOOD WITH a distinctive grain pattern, carefully cutting and arranging parts can make the difference between a plain old box and one that might be regarded as art. I like for the grain pattern to run continuously around the box corners. To achieve this effect, I simply mark the parts in order prior to cutting them from a single board. During assembly the marks tell me which boards go where. Simple marking methods help keep parts aligned throughout the building process.

For making small boxes, there are two different tablesaw methods for cutting the mitered corners: You can angle either the blade or the miter gauge to 45 degrees. I normally make this cut with the blade tilted to 45 degrees (see p. 59 for more on this method), but for this small box it's quick and easy to angle your miter gauge. Leave the blade set at 90 degrees and raised to the full height of the box sides. I use an aftermarket miter guide on my saw (because it has positive, accurate stops to assure that it is at 45 degrees), but the stock gauge on most saws will work fine. This technique works well on box sides low enough for the saw to handle in a single pass, and it comes in handy when you're reluctant to adjust the arbor of the saw to 45 degrees.

Mitering the box sides this way requires carefully checking the angle of both the miter gauge and the blade. After setting the saw, I make a test cut on scrap wood, then check the results using a combination square **(PHOTO A)**. If adjustments need to be made, it's better to do so before cutting actual box parts.

TEST THE ANGLE Using wide stock for a trial run is a good way to test the accuracy of the miter angle. Once cut, hold the two miters against a square and check for gaps on the inside or outside of the joint.

CLEAR MARKS PREVENT MISTAKES
Mark the stock in pencil to help you reassemble the sides with matching corners. An inverted "V" points to the top of the stock. The sides can be numbered, marked front, left, back, and right, or just marked with a squiggled line from end to end.

1. To lay out the box sides, mark the top of the stock to denote the approximate cut lines, allowing ¼ in. to ⅜ in. of waste between cuts. This wiggle room allows for slight inaccuracy in the initial cuts but has little effect on the matching grain at the box corners. To help keep parts in order, mark out an inverted "V" on the sides, pointing to the top edge on the face side of each piece. I also make a squiggle line through the length of the stock. During assembly, this squiggle helps keep the parts in order **(PHOTO B)**. All of the pencil marks are sanded away after the box is assembled.

2. Begin cutting the parts to rough length by cutting a miter at one end of each side piece. To help align parts and reduce waste, it helps to make a mark on the throat plate of the saw that denotes the cut line **(PHOTO C)**.

C

MITER ONE END Cut each of the right-hand miters, leaving the stock slightly oversize in length. Note the mark on the tablesaw insert that helps in aligning the stock for the first cut. Align the cut mark on the stock with the line on the tablesaw insert.

WORK SMART

Even the small width of a pencil line can make the difference between sloppy work and perfectly fitted joints. But by using jigs, sleds, and stop blocks you can alleviate the errors easily. Rather than risk inaccuracies from marking on stock with a pencil or knife and then aligning it with the sawblade, simply measure from the edge of the sawblade to the stop block.

D

STOP BLOCKS ENSURE ACCURACY
Use a stop block clamped in place on the miter gauge to cut each box side to length. This box is square, so each cut is made with the stop block in the same position.

3. To cut miters on the opposite ends of the sides, use a piece of scrap clamped to the miter gauge as a stop block. Using a clamp to hold the stock is both safer and more accurate than trying to hold the small pieces with your hand. Not only does it get your hands out of the way, but it also applies enough pressure to hold the stock in place throughout the cut. C-clamps or quick-release clamps work well—just be sure to place the clamp so that it won't interfere with the path of the blade **(PHOTO D)**.

CUTTING A PERFECT MITER

When cutting miter joints there are two common but easily avoided errors that lead to sloppy joints. The first is in the accuracy of the angle. The second which is often overlooked, is the length of the box sides. If the length of each side doesn't perfectly match its mate on the opposite side, no amount of precision in setting the angle can compensate. You will note throughout this book that I rely on stop blocks for controlling the accurate length of parts, achieving a level of accuracy that is hard to match when measuring and marking multiple parts with a pencil.

To double-check the angle cut for miters, I use a simple technique shown in photo on p. 9. Using wide stock to test the angle, even for thin sides, makes the discrepancies easily apparent. Another popular technique is to miter four pieces equal in length and check that the angle closes at all corners. If one or more corners shows a small space at the inside, either the angle of the blade or the miter gauge should be decreased very slightly.

If the corners appear slightly open on the outside, increase the angle very slightly. It can be aggravating to go through trial and error every time you change the arbor setting of the saw or the exact angle of the miter gauge, so when you get it just right, adjust and tighten the angle stops on your miter gauge. For greater accuracy, consider buying an aftermarket miter gauge—it's an investment that you won't regret.

A PERFECT FIT Aim for miters that go together without gaps on the inside or outside of the corners. It is satisfying when the first trial assembly shows miters that fit this well. Cutting a test miter in wider stock will help to assure a perfect fit even before the first side is cut.

4. Once the joints are cut, dry-assemble the box sides and check the accuracy of the miters. A perfect fit will have no voids on either the inside or the outside of the miter **(PHOTO E)**.

Fit the box bottom

USING PLYWOOD FOR THE BOTTOM OF THIS box allows you to forget about the seasonal wood movement that occurs with hardwoods. I used ¼-in. Baltic birch plywood, but all plywoods offer more stability than hardwoods. By housing the plywood bottom in a groove, it's easy to keep the entire assembly square during glue-up. Gluing the bottom in place also adds strength to the box.

KERF THE SIDES A single pass over the blade cuts saw kerfs in the box sides to house the bottom. Use your left hand to hold the parts against the fence and keep your right hand on the push block to guide the wood through the cut.

MEASURE THE GROOVE Use a tape measure to determine the size of the box bottom. Subtract $\frac{1}{64}$ in. to $\frac{1}{32}$ in. to ease the fit.

1. Start by cutting a $\frac{1}{8}$-in. saw kerf in the lower portion of each box side. Pay close attention to the inverted "V" markings on the box sides. For making this cut, the "V" should be visible and pointing away from the tablesaw fence. I use a $\frac{1}{8}$-in.-kerf combination blade, which makes a nice flat-bottomed cut, but any $\frac{1}{8}$-in.-kerf blade will work. Raise the blade $\frac{3}{16}$ in. above the surface of the saw and set the fence so that it measures $\frac{1}{4}$ in. to the outside of the blade. I use $\frac{1}{4}$-in.-thick plywood—on edge and against the fence—as a quick measuring aid. Use a push block to guide the box sides across the saw (**PHOTO A**).

2. To achieve a perfect fit for the bottom, you're better off measuring the actual parts in hand than blindly following the measurements given in the Materials List on p. 5. To determine the length and width of the bottom, measure the full width of the deepest part of the grooves cut in the box sides (**PHOTO B**). Because this is a square box, the length should be the same as the width. Reduce the measurement by $\frac{1}{64}$ in. to $\frac{1}{32}$ in. to ease the fit as the box is assembled.

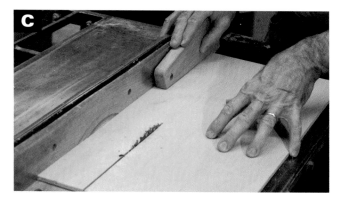

RIP THE BOTTOM TO SIZE Use the tablesaw and fence to rip the $\frac{1}{4}$-in. Baltic birch bottom to width. The blade should be lowered so that the height of the cut is $\frac{1}{8}$ in. to $\frac{1}{4}$ in. above the thickness of the stock.

CROSSCUT TO WIDTH Use a miter gauge or crosscut sled to cut the bottom to length. A stop block assures the accuracy of the cut.

3. To size the bottom, rip the plywood to width at the tablesaw **(PHOTO C)**. Then cut the bottoms to length using the miter gauge. Clamping a stop block in place helps to accurately control the length. Even if you are only making one box, this production technique provides greater accuracy— and it's a lot safer than trying to crosscut such a short piece against the fence **(PHOTO D)**.

4. To form the tongue that fits into the grooves on the sides, adjust the fence so that there is ⅛ in. between the fence and the blade. Rather than going by measurements alone, I begin making this cut with the blade a bit low and adjust gradually to achieve a perfect fit **(PHOTO E)**.

RABBET THE BOTTOM Use the tablesaw to cut the tongues on the box bottoms. The space between the blade and fence must equal the width of the saw kerf cut in the box sides. Making a test cut on scrap stock is the easiest way to check your settings.

Assemble the box

CARE MUST BE TAKEN DURING ASSEMBLY to keep the parts in order and the grain patterns continuous around the corners. This is where the squiggle line comes in handy, particularly for woods with a subtle grain pattern.

1. Begin by laying out the parts in the order of assembly, with their outer faces up on the bench. You'll flip the pieces over as the glue is applied **(PHOTO A)**.

RUBBER BANDS MAKE PERFECT CLAMPS Lay out parts to make certain that the corners match, then spread glue on each of the mitered surfaces. Large rubber bands provide sufficient clamping pressure when the joints fit well. Additional rubber bands can be added to increase clamping pressure.

An alternate method of assembly that is equally effective is to use tape. This is a favorite technique among my students. Simply lay the parts out in order and put tape where the sides meet. Apply glue to all the mitered surfaces, roll the box around the bottom, and apply tape to the last corner. Additional layers of tape increase the pressure on the joints, holding them securely as the glue dries. One advantage of using clear tape is that you can see marks on the box during assembly, and it's easy to check the alignment of the grain. If any adhesive is left on the wood once the tape is removed, a light sanding prior to finishing will remove it.

CLAMP UP WITH TAPE Lay out the box sides in order, then tape the joints with clear package tape. Apply glue to the joints, inset the bottom, and roll the sides around the bottom.

2. Spread glue carefully onto each mitered surface. Also, place a dab of glue in the groove used to house the bottom. If you are using a hardwood bottom this glue should be avoided, but in this box the plywood bottom reinforces the joint and makes miter keys unnecessary in the lower sides of the box.

3. On mitered boxes as small as these there is no better way to clamp parts together than to use rubber bands. The amount of clamping pressure is less important than keeping the parts held firmly in position while the glue sets. The rubber bands are easy to adjust, allowing you to tweak the alignment of the joints before the glue begins to set. You can add more rubber bands if needed, each layer overlapping previous ones until you've built up enough pressure to close the joints. For an alternative assembly method, see "Assembling with Tape," above.

4. Measure from corner to corner to check that the box is square. Measurements across both directions should be exactly the same. If not, a light squeeze on the long dimension is usually enough to bring the parts into alignment **(PHOTO B)**.

CHECK FOR SQUARE Develop the habit of checking to see that all your assemblies are square. If the tape measures equally from corner to corner from alternate directions, the box is square.

Add keys to the corners

INSERTING KEYS IN THE MITER JOINTS OF this box not only strengthens the corners, but also adds a decorative element and draws your eye toward the top of the box. I used black walnut keys to contrast with the oak sides, but using keys of the same species would lend the box a more subtle look. To cut the slots for the keys, you'll need to make a simple key-slot jig (see "Quick Jig for Key Slots" below) that rides against your table-saw fence. This easily made jig is very useful and effective for small boxes. If you expect to make a number of boxes or simply want a more versatile and long-lasting fixture, take a look at the sled on pp. 106–107.

1. After you've assembled the box and made the key-slot jig below, you're ready to start cutting key slots on the box corners. Begin by raising the table-saw blade to about ½ in. above the table.

2. Nest the box into place in the jig, using the fence to control the position of the cut.

QUICK JIG FOR KEY SLOTS

Cutting the miter key slots for small boxes requires a simple and effective jig that should take under five minutes to make. You'll only need a scrap piece of ¼-in. plywood or MDF (about 3½ in. wide and 16 in. long) and a 12-in. length of 2×4.

1. Use the tablesaw to cut the 2×4 at a 45-degree angle somewhere near the middle of the board. Accuracy of the angle is important but the exact placement of the cut is not (**PHOTO A**).

GLUE UP THE JIG Arrange the angled pieces to make a cradle, the add glue to attach the back.

CUT THE ANGLE Use the miter gauge to cut angles on 2×4 stock.

2. Cut a piece of ¼-in. plywood to the same width as the 2×4 and approximately the same length as the 2×4 laid out (**PHOTO B**).

3. Spread glue on one face of each 2×4. Carefully align the plywood and attach it with brad nails. Keep the nails outside of the area that is to be cut (**PHOTO C**).

3. Make a cut at each corner, rotating the box between cuts. Care should be taken to hold the box and jig tightly to the fence throughout the cuts. Letting the box slip slightly can cause a wider cut and lead to a poor-fitting key slot.

4. Move the fence ¼ in. further from the blade to cut the second set of slots. To give the design a more interesting decorative effect, these slots aren't as deep as the first ones. To make shallower cuts, lower the blade slightly, about ⅛ in. **(PHOTO A)**.

CUT THE KEY SLOTS Cradle the box in the key-slot jig, and while holding the box and jig tightly against the fence, pass them across the blade. Rotate the box between cuts to make key slots at all four corners.

NAIL IT IN PLACE When securing the back to the cradle, take care to place nails out of the path of the blade.

To use the jig, place the box within the "V." Hold the box and jig tightly against the fence, then push them through the blade. After making multiple cuts in multiple spots on this jig, the underside will get a little worn out—take five minutes to make another, or invest your time and materials building the long-lasting jig shown on p. 106 in the Fold-Out Jewelry Box project.

Key-slot jig

This easy-to-build jig makes cutting key slots fast work at the tablesaw. To make one, you'll need only a scrap of 2x4 and a little plywood or medium density fiberboard (MDF).

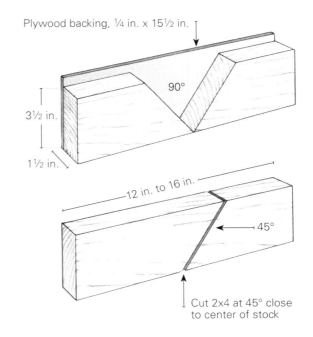

Plywood backing, ¼ in. x 15½ in.

90°

3½ in.

1½ in.

12 in. to 16 in.

45°

Cut 2x4 at 45° close to center of stock

CUT THE MITER-KEY STOCK
Use the tablesaw to cut ⅛-in. stock
for making miter keys. Perfectly
sizing the keys usually requires some
trial and error. Test the fit in the key
slots, and discard strips that fit either
too tightly or too loosely.

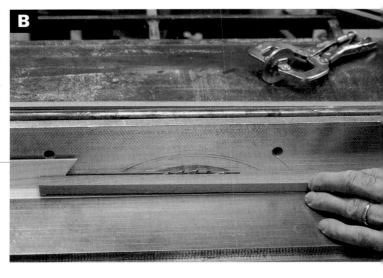

Cutting the keys

1. To make the keys, start with stock that is ⅛-in. wider than the deepest key slot. At the tablesaw, rip thin strips from that stock. Use a splitter to help control the thin stock through the cut, and have a push stick ready to finish the cut. Check the fit of your strips as they come off the saw and discard strips that are too loose (**PHOTO B**). I prefer keys that fit slightly tight, but if you have to use more than finger pressure or a slight tap to fit them into the kerf, you risk breaking the joint open.

2. One of the easiest ways to cut the strips into triangular keys is to use a quick-sawing jig like the one shown below (**PHOTO C**), but they could also be cut using a miter gauge on the tablesaw or bandsaw. I use a Japanese dozuki saw for a smooth quick cut with the jig. Clamp the jig in the vise or to your benchtop and make the first cut. To form the triangular keys, slide the stock down, flip it over, and make another cut.

Miter key jig

When building this miter jig, use a wide board for the base so that you can clamp the jig to the bench top. Alternately, nail a strip onto the underside so you can clamp the whole assembly into a vise.

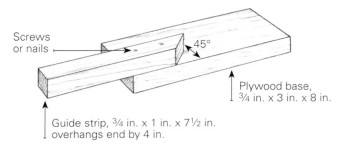

Screws or nails

45°

Plywood base, ¾ in. x 3 in. x 8 in.

Guide strip, ¾ in. x 1 in. x 7½ in. overhangs end by 4 in.

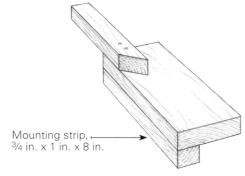

Mounting strip, ¾ in. x 1 in. x 8 in.

CUT THE KEYS TO SHAPE Cut one end at a 45-degree angle, then flip the piece over and make the second cut to form the key. Keep flipping and cutting and in a matter of minutes you will have made enough keys for several boxes.

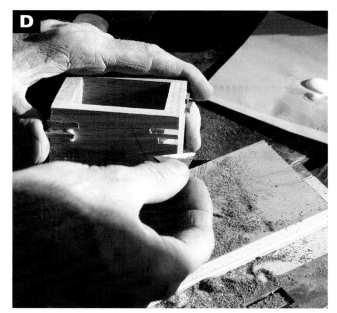

INSERT THE KEYS Spread a bit of glue on the leading edge of the keys, then slip them into place.

SAND THE KEYS FLUSH WITH SIDES Use a stationary belt sander to sand the keys flush with the surrounding box sides. Sanding by hand is a little slower, but it works as well.

3. To install the keys, spread glue on the top, bottom, and long flat edge of each, then press them into place. If a key is too tight to press in place with your fingers, give it a tap with a small hammer. If it takes more than a slight tap, however, you run the risk of breaking the glued joint. It may also be helpful to hammer the keys slightly on a flat surface, compressing them before fitting. Moisture in the glue will cause the keys to swell to their original thickness once they're installed **(PHOTO D)**.

4. Use a stationary belt sander to sand the keys flush with the box sides. This job can also easily be done by hand with a sanding block, or by working the box across a flat piece of coarse sandpaper affixed to the surface of a workbench **(PHOTO E)**.

Make a lift lid

LID DETAILS ARE ONE OF THE MANY WAYS to personalize this box, and for more variations on this same design, see "Design Options" on p. 22. To make the lid, you can choose between various woods, selected for their beauty and character. For variety, I cut the lids for these boxes from curly maple, figured walnut, spalted maple, and coarsely textured walnut with an extremely rough-sawn side

that shows signs of exposure to wind, rain, and sun during the process of air drying.

1. To make the ¾-in.-thick lid, begin by cutting it to size using the same tablesaw methods you used to cut the bottom. Rip the planed stock to width and then use either the tablesaw miter gauge or a crosscut sled (see the box in "Rustic Treasure Box"

FIT THE TOP Use the router table and a straight bit to rabbet the lid. Rout the end grain first so that the routing of the side grain will remove any tearout resulting from the first cuts.

CUT THE TOP TO SHAPE To cut the top to a more interesting shape, angle the tablesaw blade to 9 degrees. Leave enough edge on the sides of the lid to follow the fence during each cut.

on pp. 28–29) to cut it to length. Even if you are making only one lid, ripping longer stock is safer than trying to cut a single lid from a small board.

2. Cut a lip along the underside of the top using a router table and straight-cut router bit. Using the router table allows you to adjust the fence (and the width of the lip) in small increments until the base of the top fits snugly inside the box. For the best results, use the widest straight-cut

router bit you have. My preferred bit is 1¼ in. in diameter, but a ¾-in. or 1-in. diameter bit would work also **(PHOTO A)**.

3. There are an infinite variety of attractive ways to shape the lid for this box. As an example, use the tablesaw with the blade tilted to 8 or 9 degrees and cut the lid to shape by passing it between the blade and the fence **(PHOTO B)**.

Final touches

ONCE THE BOX IS ASSEMBLED, IT'S WORTH taking a few extra steps to give it a more refined look. I use a 45-degree chamfering bit in the router table to rout the bottom edge of the box **(PHOTO A)**, but the same effect could be achieved with a block plane or a coarse sanding block. I prefer to do most of the final sanding on an inverted half-sheet sander—it's a lot less work than sanding by hand. I begin sanding with a stationary belt sander using 100 and 150 grits. For the final sanding, I use an inverted half-sheet sander progressing through 180, 240, and 320 grit. Hand-sanding would also work **(PHOTO B on facing page)**.

On this box I used a Danish oil finish because I love the way it brings well-sanded wood to life. Pay close attention to the directions on the can. As a general rule, I flood the surface of the wood with a generous first application. I use a brush to reach the inside corners of the box and then use a bit of rag to wipe the sides and lid. I keep the surface wet for about an hour before rubbing it out. Torn up cloth from an old cotton shirt is an excellent material for wiping down the oil before it is fully dried. In rubbing out the finish, the objective is to keep spreading the finish around evenly into the pores of the wood. The second application builds to a higher gloss, but dries more quickly. Be watchful on the second and third coats and make sure that you don't let the finish become tacky before rubbing it out. Usually, the second and third coats need only half the time of the first coat before rubbing out (**PHOTO C**).

B

SAND TO 320 GRIT An inverted half-sheet sander clamped to the workbench is used to smooth small boxes in a short amount of time.

APPLY THE FINISH
A Danish oil finish brings the wood to life. Old T-shirts make good rags for rubbing out. Spread out oily rags to dry flat before throwing them away.

C

CHAMFER THE BOTTOM Use a chamfering bit in the router table to shape the bottom edges of the box. If you prefer, rounds, coves, or other router profiles can be used instead.

There are many ways to personalize this box. You can alter almost any aspect of this box—size, wood choices, or joinery techniques.

ONE EASY WAY TO ACHIEVE A DRAMATICALLY different look is to use dowels rather than keys to reinforce the miter joints **(PHOTO A)**. The first step is to drill holes to accommodate the dowels. Use a drill press outfitted with a fence and stop blocks to set the exact locations for the holes. At each corner, drill two dowels from one side and a single hole centered on the adjacent side **(PHOTO B)**. To cut the short dowels to length, I use a tablesaw sled outfitted with a stop block, then hold the offcut in place using the eraser end of a pencil **(PHOTO C)**. If you're only cutting a few dowels, however, a handsaw works fine. Sand the box thoroughly before installing the dowels. Use sandpaper to soften the edges of the dowels, then drive them in place with a tack hammer. If the fit is tight, you won't need any glue.

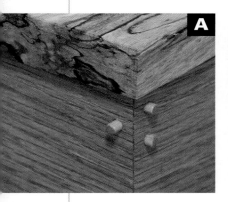

Making the lid from a figured or contrasting species of wood or cutting it to a slightly different shape are two other easy ways to lend this box a new look. For the roughsawn walnut lids I rabbeted the underside to fit the box and then chamfered the lower edges with a stationary belt sander. A light cleaning with a stiff brush to loosen dirt followed by the application of an oil finish allowed it to tell its own interesting story. Burled and figured woods like the maple and walnut lids are well featured when used in the making of this box.

CUT THE DOWELS TO LENGTH (ABOVE RIGHT) Either a tablesaw sled or a handsaw can be used to cut the dowels to length. Here, a stop block controls the length and the eraser end of a pencil is used to keep the small pieces from being thrown by the saw.

DRILL THE BOX TO ACCEPT DOWELS (ABOVE CENTER) For a slightly different look, dowels are used to reinforce the corner joints. A 1/8-in. dowel is a good choice for small boxes like these. A drill press outfitted with a fence is used to drill holes that are perfectly spaced from the edge and uniform in depth.

A Rustic Treasure Box

THIS BOX IS DESIGNED in remembrance of the pleasure I found in the small boxes I had as a child. Make one for a child, grandchild, or even yourself and you can tap into some of what I felt. This particular design evolved from treasure boxes made by first through fourth graders at the school where I teach woodworking. But this box uses techniques better suited to adult box makers.

Rabbeted corners make this box easy to assemble, and the floating bottom panel all but assures that the box will go together square. Reinforcing the rabbeted corners with dowels strengthens the joinery—you can expect this box to be around for generations. But perhaps my favorite part of this box is the leather hinge. The leather hinge on this box is perfectly in keeping with its rustic character, and its design is based on the type of intertwined hinge that is used in making a once-common child's toy, the "Jacob's Ladder."

Rustic box with leather hinge

Made of white oak, this rustic box is held together using simple rabbet joints that are reinforced with small dowels. The leather hinge is made from three interlocking pieces of scrap leather that are cut, glued, and nailed in place. The hinge also provides a built-in stop at 90°.

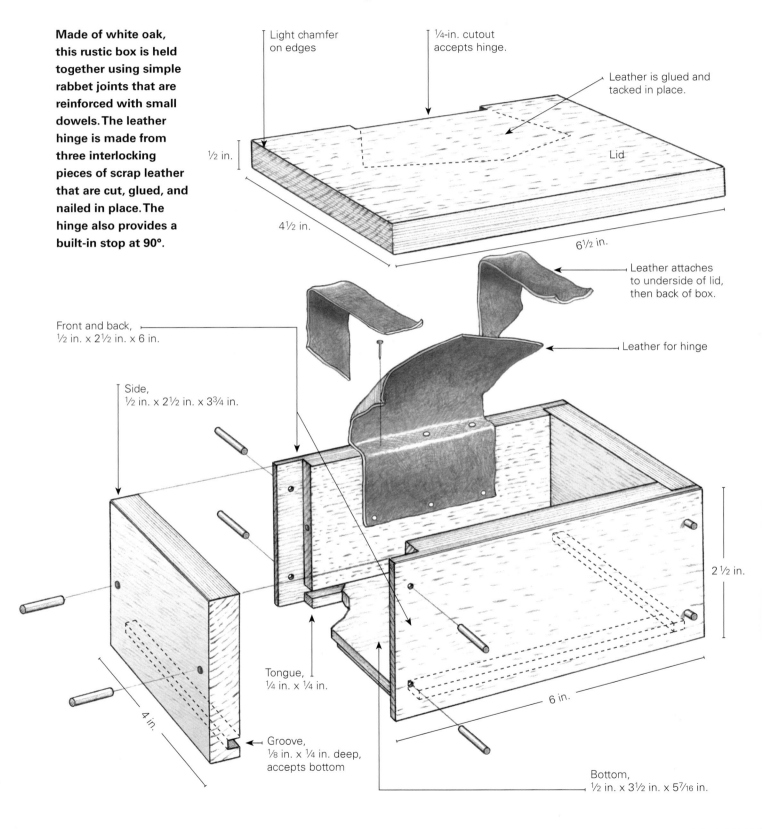

Light chamfer on edges

¼-in. cutout accepts hinge.

Leather is glued and tacked in place.

½ in.

Lid

4½ in.

6½ in.

Leather attaches to underside of lid, then back of box.

Front and back, ½ in. x 2½ in. x 6 in.

Leather for hinge

Side, ½ in. x 2½ in. x 3¾ in.

2 ½ in.

Tongue, ¼ in. x ¼ in.

4 in.

6 in.

Groove, ⅛ in. x ¼ in. deep, accepts bottom

Bottom, ½ in. x 3½ in. x 5⁷⁄₁₆ in.

Detail of Rabbet Joint

½ in.

³⁄₈ in.

Hinge Detail

Pivots here →

Leather

Leather hinge

RUSTIC TREASURE BOX MATERIALS

QUANTITY	PART	ACTUAL SIZE	CONSTRUCTION NOTES
2	Front and back	½ in. × 2½ in. × 6¹⁄₁₆ in.*	White oak
2	Ends	½ in. × 2½ in. × 3¾ in.	White oak
2	Lid	½ in. × 4½ in. × 6½ in.	Quartersawn white oak
16	⅛-in.-dia. hardwood dowels	⅛ in. × ⅞ in. long	Sand ends before installation
1	Leather scrap	6-in. square	Available from www.tandyleather.com

*Length includes ¹⁄₃₂-in. cleanup allowance at each end.

Cut the parts to size

THE MOST IMPORTANT THING IN CUTTING the parts to size is that opposite sides of the box match in length. To achieve this level of precision, use a crosscut sled with a stop block clamped in place. If you don't already have a crosscut sled, it's worth investing the small amount of time it takes to make one. For more on tablesaw sleds, see "Making a Crosscut Sled" on pp. 28–29.

1. At the tablesaw, use a crosscut sled to square one end of each piece of stock. Even if the stock was cut square prior to planing and jointing, these simple operations may have altered the stock enough to require squaring the end again. A little insurance never hurts.

2. Measure and mark the length of the long sides (the front and back) on your crosscut sled, then clamp a stop block in place at that mark. Though you cut the front and back one at a time, using a stop block assures that both cuts will match perfectly **(PHOTO )**.

3. After cutting the front and back, change the location of the stop block to cut the shorter ends.

WORK SMART

A zero-clearance insert (as seen in photo B) allows you to cut boards on edge or remove small offcuts at the tablesaw. Whether you make them yourself or buy inserts to fit your saw, they will provide much greater flexibility, safety, and accuracy.

A

CUT THE SIDES TO LENGTH Using a crosscut sled with a stop block clamped in place guarantees that matching parts are identical in length. Don't forget to trim and square one end first, cutting away any knots or unsound material.

Cut the corner joints

A

BEGIN CUTTING RABBET JOINT
Set the stop block so that the distance between the outside edge of the blade and the stop block equals the thickness of the stock plus a little more, to be sanded away after assembly. The height of the cut above the surface of the sled should be ³⁄₈ in.

CUTTING THE RABBETED JOINT REQUIRES only two steps on the tablesaw. The first cut is made with the stock laying flat on the sled, and the second cut is made with the stock standing on end with one face against the fence.

1. Raise the blade on the tablesaw ³⁄₈ in. above the base of the sled. Because your stock is ½ in. thick, this will leave ⅛ in. of the stock uncut. If you've got scrap of the same thickness, it's a good idea to make a test cut.

2. Adjust the stop block on the sled so that the distance from the stop block to the far side of the blade is a hair thicker than the stock you're cutting. This will provide for a small lip to be sanded away after assembly. Once you're satisfied with the results on your test piece, cut both the front and back of the box with the stock laying flat on the sled (**PHOTO A**).

3. To finish forming the rabbet, start by removing the sled, setting the blade height to ½ in., and adjusting the space between the blade and fence to ⅛ in. Once the settings are dialed in, guide your stock—on edge and against the fence—through the blade. For safety, be sure you have a zero-clearance insert in place on your tablesaw (**PHOTO B**).

B

FINISH THE RABBET JOINT
When guiding stock vertically against the fence, be sure to keep your fingers clear of the blade's path. A zero-clearance insert is required to support the stock throughout the cut.

One of the most important discoveries in my own box making was the tablesaw sled. My sleds are lighter in weight and easier to use than the common sleds many craftsmen use, and I make them for a variety of specific uses, increasing the overall accuracy and efficiency of my work.

Sleds are much safer to use than traditional miter gauges. Many tablesaw injuries result from small offcuts being picked up and thrown by the blade; more serious injuries result from reaching into the blade to remove offcut stock. The natural motion of the sled into and then back away from the cut allows you to remove stock without putting your hands near the blade (**PHOTO A**). You will see a variety of sleds used in the course of this book, and despite some variations in their design, all start on common ground. The basics given here will remain true for all of the sleds used in this book.

The trickiest part of making a sled is installing the runners. They must be parallel to the blade and move smoothly in the miter-gauge slots on your saw table.

SLEDS ARE SAFER Sleds allow you to pull small parts safely away from the blade before removing them.

Basic crosscut sled

This sled is both safer and more accurate than the miter gauge that comes with most tablesaws. It's also fast and easy to make.

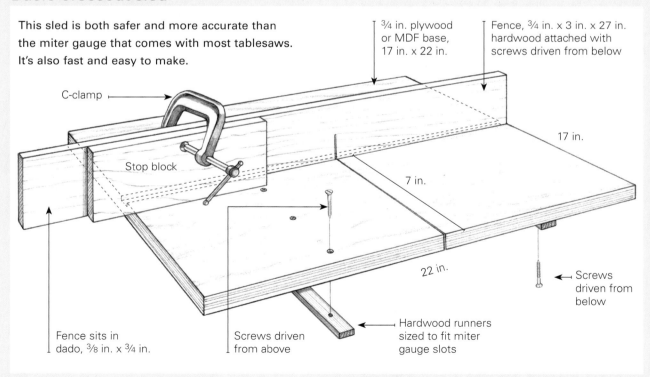

C-clamp

Stop block

Fence sits in
dado, ⅜ in. x ¾ in.

Screws driven
from above

¾ in. plywood
or MDF base,
17 in. x 22 in.

Fence, ¾ in. x 3 in. x 27 in.
hardwood attached with
screws driven from below

17 in.

7 in.

22 in.

Screws
driven from
below

Hardwood runners
sized to fit miter
gauge slots

1. Start with a rectangular piece of plywood and two pieces of hardwood (one for the fence and another to form both runners). It helps if the plywood is square at all four corners, but this technique works as long as it has one straight edge.

FIT THE FENCE TO THE BASE Plane the fence stock to a thickness that fits snug in the dado. Alternately, you could widen the dado to fit already-planed stock.

2. Use a ¾-in.-wide dado blade in the tablesaw to make a dado cut ⅜ in. deep about 8 in. from the edge of the plywood. Plane the stock for the fence to fit in the dado. Alternately, you can widen the dado cut to accept the stock you're using for your fence. Aim for a fit that is snug **(PHOTO B)**.

ATTACH THE RUNNER TO THE BASE After milling the runner to fit in the miter-gauge slot, attach it to the base with a single screw. Square the runner to the back of the sled, then add screws down the length of the runner.

3. To make the runners, plane hardwood stock to fit the miter-guide slots in the tablesaw top.

4. Attach the first runner with a single screw and countersink it in place on the underside of the plywood base. Use a square to make certain that the runner is square to the edge you ran against the fence when you cut the dado. Holding the runner tightly in place, add two more screws **(PHOTO C)**.

5. Flip the sled base over and set the runner you just attached into the miter-gauge slot. Slide the second runner in place and use 1-in. drywall screws to attach it from above **(PHOTO D)**.

6. Attach the fence using 1⅝-in. screws driven in from the underside. Don't position any screws where they'll interfere with the path of the blade **(PHOTO E)**.

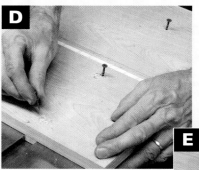

ADD THE SECOND RUNNER Fit the first sled runner into the tablesaw guide slot and place the second runner in the other slot. Use screws to attach the second runner from above.

ATTACH THE FENCE The fence is attached to the base using screws driven from underneath.

Make and fit the bottom

UNLIKE PLYWOOD, SOLID WOOD EXPANDS and contracts with seasonal changes in humidity. Beginning woodworkers often try to deny this fact, but you'll be better off once you learn to accept it and then design around it. The floating bottom of this box is designed to expand and contract freely without breaking open the corner joints of the box. Tongues cut on the edges of the bottom fit into the grooves on the sides of the box, and the bottom is sized to allow for a small amount of expansion.

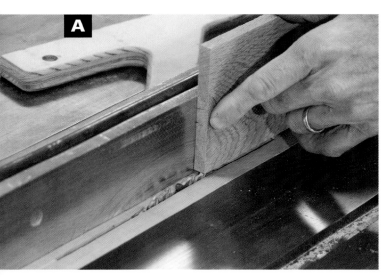

SET UP USING THE STOCK, NOT A RULER Because the side is grooved to accommodate the thickness of the bottom, adjust the fence setting directly from the stock.

1. Set the saw fence so that the distance between the fence and the outside of the blade is equal to the thickness of the box bottom. For results that are more precise than you'll get from a ruler or tape measure, hold the bottom on edge and against the fence. Align the edge of the stock with the outside of the blade, then lock the fence in position. For safety, be sure to install a zero clearance insert (**PHOTO A**).

2. Lower the blade height to cut only a hair over ¼ in. above the surface of the tablesaw. With the stock laying flat on the saw, cut a groove in the front, back, and ends of the box. Once the box is assembled, the groove that houses the bottom panel will be hidden from view by the overlap for the rabbet joint at the corners of the box (**PHOTO B**).

3. Check the actual dimensions of the interior of the box, then rip and crosscut the bottom to size. When calculating the dimensions of the bottom, don't forget to add the depth of the grooves on each side. To allow for wood expansion during humid conditions, cut the bottom panel about ¹⁄₆₄ in. shorter in length and about ¹⁄₃₂ in. narrower than the actual measurements. I rip the stock to width using the rip fence, then use a sled outfitted with a stop block to cut the length (**PHOTO C**).

GROOVE THE SIDES TO ACCEPT THE BOTTOM Use a ⅛-in. combination blade to cut grooves in each of the box sides. Pass the front and back across the blade with the rabbeted sides down, then make the same cuts on the ends.

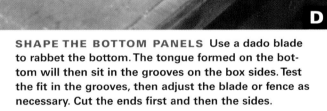

SHAPE THE BOTTOM PANELS Use a dado blade to rabbet the bottom. The tongue formed on the bottom will then sit in the grooves on the box sides. Test the fit in the grooves, then adjust the blade or fence as necessary. Cut the ends first and then the sides.

4. To cut the tongue on the bottom, install a dado blade set to ¼ in. wide. Raise the blade to ¼ in. and set the fence ⅛ in. from the inside of the blade. Cut the tongues with the stock held vertically against the fence. Be sure to use a zero-clearance insert so that the tongue is fully supported throughout the cut. Cut the end grain first. Cutting across end grain usually results in tearout, so cutting the side grain last will clean up the cut **(PHOTO D)**.

CUT THE BOX BOTTOMS After squaring one end, use a sled outfitted with a stop block to cut the bottoms to length.

Assemble the box

IT IS MUCH EASIER TO SAND THE INTERIOR surfaces of the box before you put it together. Prior to assembly, you'll also need to attach the leather hinge to the inner face at the back of the box. The leather hinge consists of three parts: A large center piece attaches to the inside of the back and stretches over the back of the lid and onto the top, and two side strips stretch from the inside of the lid to the back of the box. At this point, you only need to attach the center piece to the inside back of the box. The side strips will be added later. There are no exact requirements for the shape of the leather except that the edges where it passes through the back of the box need to be straight. Refer to the drawing on pp. 24–25 for details, then cut the leather using scissors. Center the leather on the inside of the back of the box. Once the hinge is in place, you're ready to assemble the box. Start by gluing up the box, then add reinforcing dowels to the corner joints after the glue has cured.

1. Spread hot-melt glue on the leather and then use tacks to hold it securely in place. If you use copper tacks, which bend easily, you'll find it helpful to predrill before driving the tacks in place. Regular steel tacks are much easier to drive into most hardwoods (**PHOTO A**).

ASSEMBLE THE BOX Spread glue on the inside surface of the rabbet prior to assembly. First glue one joint and place the bottom in position, then glue the other three corners.

BEGIN INSTALLING THE LEATHER HINGE Before assembling the box, install the center portion of the leather hinge using both glue and tacks. If you're using copper tacks, you'll need to predrill the holes. Cut steel tacks can be hammered into most hardwoods.

WORK SMART

Learning to apply the right amount of glue is a skill that develops over time. End grain absorbs more glue than cross-grain and requires a heavier application. The tendency with beginners is to apply too much glue and make a mess, but practice and careful attention lead to a lot less cleanup.

2. The box should go together easily. Begin by spreading yellow glue in each of the four rabbets. Use a little extra glue on the end grain. No glue is required on the bottom, as it should be allowed to float freely in response to changes in humidity. If you wish, a dab of glue at the center on each end of the panel can be used to keep the bottom centered in the box. Glue one end to one long side, slip the bottom in place, and then add the other end and side (**PHOTO B**).

3. Use rubber bands to hold the box together as the glue dries. Apply enough rubber bands to make sure the joints all close up across their length. You really can't use too many rubber bands—additional bands only add to the clamping pressure. Before the glue sets, be sure to check to see that the box is square: Measure corner to corner across both diagonals and make adjustments until the measurements are the same. To make adjustments, simply give the box a squeeze across the long diagonal and check again (**PHOTO C**).

CLAMP THE BOX Rubber bands supply sufficient pressure to hold the box together while the glue dries. Check to see that the box is square by measuring from corner to corner in both directions. If both measurements are the same, the box is square.

Add a lid

THE LID OF THIS BOX IS CUT FROM A SOLID piece of quartersawn stock. Quartersawn material is much less prone to warping because its expansion and contraction tends to be uniform across the grain. For this reason, quartersawn material is almost always the best choice for solid wood lids. By making the lid large enough to overhang all four sides of the box, the lid has a positive stop in the open position. A shallow relief cut across the back allows clearance for attaching the hinge.

1. Place the lid in position on the box, then mark the location of the leather hinge on the rear edge of the lid.

It is difficult to hold very small parts with adult fingers. Use needle-nose pliers to hold small parts in position, then tap them into place. If you're concerned that you'll damage the part, use a short dowel to cushion the hammer blows as you drive it into place.

2. Raise the tablesaw blade to cut ¼ in. above the surface of the sled, then make a series of cuts through the edge of the lid stock where the hinge will sit **(PHOTO A)**. Aim for a flat cut across the back of the box. Note in **PHOTO B** how the leather fits snugly in the relief cut into the back of the lid.

FIT THE HINGE The leather should fit snugly in the space formed by the saw-cuts across the back of the lid. If necessary, trim the hinge to size with scissors.

CUT THE LID TO ACCEPT THE HINGE The recess at the back of the lid allows clearance for the center part of the leather hinge. Mark out the hinge location on the back of the lid, then create the recess by making a series of cuts using your tablesaw sled.

3. Gently shape the front edge of the lid using a sanding disk. Mark a guide point ⅛ in. in from each of the front corners and sand lightly from the center to the guide points **(PHOTO C)**. This will give the treasure box a subtle curve that is in keeping with the curves inherent in the leather.

SHAPE THE LID Use a disk sander to shape the lid. Make a pencil mark ⅛ in. in from each direction on each corner, then sand a curved transition from the center of the lid to the pencil marks.

Prepare for final assembly

USE THE DRILL PRESS TO PREDRILL HOLES for the dowels used to strengthen the corners. Drill into the ends of the box first, then adjust the table on the drill press to drill into the fronts and backs of the rabbeted corners. Drill to a depth of about ¾ in. If you're careful in setting the depth, you'll be able to cut all the dowels to a uniform length **(PHOTO A)**.

1. Chamfer the bottom of the box using a 45-degree chamfering bit on the router table. Rout a light chamfer on the upper and lower edges of the lid as well.

DRILL FOR DOWELS Drill the corners of the box to accept dowels, which reinforce the corner joints. Use a fence and stop blocks to control the position of the holes.

2. Sand the lid and the outside of the box. Using an inverted orbital sander saves time and muscles, but hand-sanding will work as well **(PHOTO B)**.

3. Cut the dowels to length and lightly sand their ends. Use light taps to hammer the dowels into the holes you drilled at the box corners. If the dowels fit well, there is no need to glue them in place.

4. It's easiest to finish this box before the hinge is installed on the lid. I apply two or three coats of Danish oil, rubbing the finish out between coats and building to a very slight gloss. For more on this finishing technique, see p. 21.

SAND THE LID AND OUTSIDE OF THE BOX Use an inverted orbital sander to sand the lid and the outside of the box. Move through 180 and 220 grit, then finish-sand with 240 grit. Hand-sand chamfers on the lid and bottom using a sanding block and 240 grit paper.

Attach the hinge

USE SCISSORS TO CUT LEATHER STRIPS TO fit the underside of the lid. Trim the portion of the hinge you already attached to the inside of the box, or leave it free-form for an even more rustic look.

1. To attach the hinge straps that pass from under the lid to the back of the box, use clear construction adhesive and clamps or hot-melt glue. Hot-melt glue is my preference. If the hot-melt glue cools too quickly, use an iron to give the glue additional spread. Then use tacks to secure the straps to the inside of the box lid **(PHOTO A)**.

2. Pull the leather tight into position from inside the box and glue it to the top of the lid. Then use tacks to secure it in place **(PHOTO B, on p. 36)**.

ATTACH THE SIDE STRIPS TO THE UNDERSIDE OF THE LID Leather strips glued to the underside of the lid are held in place with hot-melt glue. Once the glue sets, steel or copper tacks are tapped into place.

B

ATTACH THE CENTER STRIP TO THE TOP OF THE LID Pull the leather from the inside back of the box tight across the top of the lid. Hold the lid in position while you glue and tack the leather in place.

C

FINSIH THE HINGE Use hot melt glue to attach the leather from the underside of the lid to the back of the box, then use tacks to secure it.

3. Pull the leather strips from the underside of the lid to the back of the box. Trim the leather straps at the back of the box to an interesting shape, then pull them tight and glue and tack them in place **(PHOTO C)**.

4. For a little insurance, add tacks across the back edge of the lid. Be neat in your arrangement of the tacks so that their placement looks both intentional and decorative. A well-applied leather hinge not only looks good, but will also last a long time. Because the back of the lid overhangs the back of the box, the lid also has a built-in 90-degree stop.

DESIGN OPTIONS

Although there are numerous ways you can personalize your box, here a base and a leather latch were used.

IT IS VERY EASY TO ALTER THE SIZE OF this box, the stock used to build it, or the shape and color of the leather used for the hinges. Leave the natural edges on the leather for an even more rustic look. Other options are to add a base or install a leather latch. If you'd like to personalize the box, you can easily add a name or initials to the base or front of the box by hammering tacks into place.

ADD A BASE The base of this box is little more than a length of solid stock cut ¾ in. longer and wider than the dimensions of the box. The base is attached to the bottom of the box with wood screws.

1. Once the base is properly sized, center all four sides of the box on the base and use clamps to hold the two together.

2. Drill pilot holes through the base and into the bottom of the box, then drive in a few screws to secure it **(PHOTO A)**.

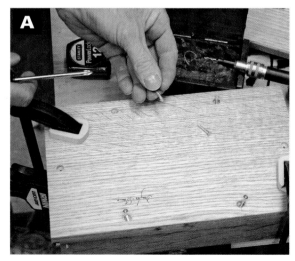

A

ATTACH A BASE Center a quartersawn base on the box, then secure it in place with screws. Screws placed too close to the corners can lead to splitting.

ATTACH A LATCH

1. To add a leather latch, cut a recess on the front of the lid in the same manner you cut hinge clearance at the back of the lid.

2. Add a leather strip that lays across the top of the lid and partially down the front of the box. Punch or cut a hole in the strip before it is nailed in place **(PHOTO B)**.

3. Mark the location of the hole with an awl. Carefully position the awl at the center of the hole in the strip and press down to create a starting point for the drill bit **(PHOTO C)**.

4. Drill a ¼-in. hole for a short dowel to fit. Note the carved notch in the dowel that helps the leather strip stay in place **(PHOTO D)**.

MAKE A CATCH A leather strap attached to the box lid wraps around the front of the box and locks onto a catch post.

DRILL AND INSTALL CATCH POST Use a ¼-in. brad-point bit to drill a hole to accept the catch post, then insert a ¼-in. dowel to serve as the post. A recess filed into the lower side of the post will catch the leather strap from the lid, locking the lid in position.

MARK FOR CATCH POST Use an awl to mark the location of the catch post.

A Sliding-Top Pencil Box

THIS SMALL BOX IS modeled after the boxes students might have used in school to hold pencils and pens. Unlike those boxes, however, this one is assembled using box joints at the corners. In this joint a set of fingers on one side of the box fits snugly into a set of fingers on the other side. A little glue locks everything into place. This strong joint can be used to make a box that will last as long as someone is willing to keep it and care for it.

This box is made using mesquite, a much admired Texas hardwood, but simply changing the wood or adjusting the size is an easy way to create boxes with a completely different look.

Box joints appear difficult to make but are actually quite easy to cut and fit. You can make box joints in a variety of sizes to complement various sizes of box by using a dado blade in place of the combination blade used to make the box joints seen here. In making this box, you'll also learn a trial-and-error process for cutting matching parts that fit together perfectly—a great addition to your skills as a woodworker.

Sliding-top box

This sliding-top box features box-jointed corners. It is made from ⅜-in. mesquite, but other woods can be substituted for equally beautiful results.

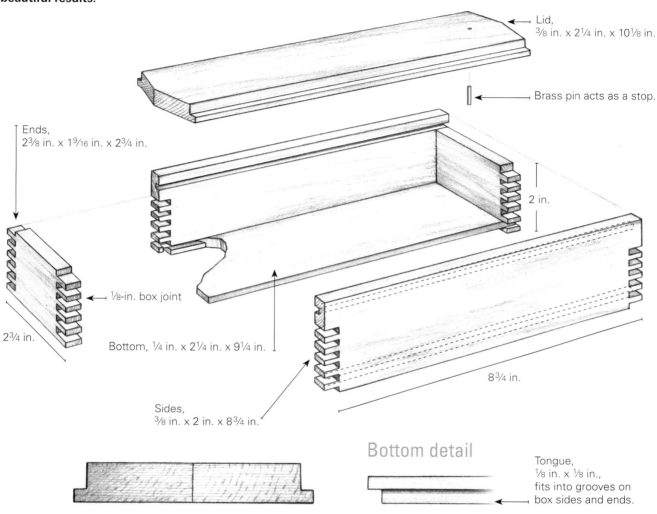

Lid,
⅜ in. x 2¼ in. x 10⅛ in.

Brass pin acts as a stop.

Ends,
2⅜ in. x 1⁹⁄₁₆ in. x 2¾ in.

2 in.

⅛-in. box joint

2¾ in.

Bottom, ¼ in. x 2¼ in. x 9¼ in.

8¾ in.

Sides,
⅜ in. x 2 in. x 8¾ in.

Bottom detail

Tongue,
⅛ in. x ⅛ in.,
fits into grooves on
box sides and ends.

MATERIALS

QUANTITY	PART	ACTUAL SIZE	CONSTRUCTION NOTES
2	Sides	⅜ in. × 2 in. × 8¹³⁄₁₆ in.*	⅜-in. mesquite
2	Ends	⅜ in. × 1⁹⁄₁₆ in. × 2¹³⁄₁₆ in.*	⅜-in. mesquite
1	Lid	⅜ in. × 2¼ in. × 10½ in.	⅜-in. mesquite
1	Bottom	¼ in. × 2¼ in. × 9¼ in.	¼-in. mesquite
1	Brass pin	⅛ in. × ⁹⁄₁₆ in.	Sand and polish ends

*Length includes an extra ¹⁄₆₄ in. at each end, to be sanded off after assembly.

Prepare the stock

CAREFUL EXAMINATION OF STOCK EARLY in a project can save you lots of headaches later on. Watch for checks and cracks in the stock, and cut away those portions of wood before starting. After selecting the stock I use a tablesaw sled to cut the box parts to size, but you could also make these cuts using only the fence and miter gauge on your saw. That said, a good crosscut sled quickly becomes a go-to jig in your shop, so it's worth taking the time to make one (See "Making a Crosscut Sled" on pp. 28–29). To make multiple cuts of exactly the same measurement, I use a stop block clamped to the tablesaw sled.

1. Rip the stock for all four sides of the box to width at the tablesaw. Be sure to keep the stock snug against the fence and to use a push stick to guide it through the cut.

2. To begin cutting the long sides to length, measure from the stop block to the tip of the sawblade, then secure the block with a small clamp. Relying on a stop block eliminates the need to mark every

CUT IT TO LENGTH Using a stop block clamped to the sled or miter gauge establishes the length of the cut and allows you to cut multiple pieces of exactly the same length.

piece to size, and does away with inaccuracies that arise from pencil markings on wood.

3. Before cutting the stock to length, trim one end square. Keep a watchful eye on splits and imperfections that might make the stock ill-suited for your box **(PHOTO A)**.

SQUARE ONE END Your fist cut should remove any defects found at the ends of the stock and provide a square starting point for cutting parts to length. Either a crosscut sled or an accurate miter gauge can be used to square the end.

4. Slide the freshly cut edge against the stop block and make the cut. As you hold the stock through the cut, be sure to keep your hands out of the path of the blade **(PHOTO B)**.

5. To cut the two ends of the box, adjust the position of the stop block, then use the same cutting methods you used on the long sides.

Cut the joints

WHEN YOU LOOK AT THEM, BOX JOINTS seem like they would be very difficult to cut, but with a tablesaw and an easily made jig, it's simple work. The quickly made jig attaches to either a tablesaw sled or your saw's standard miter gauge. The sled, because it has two runners rather than just one, tends to offer greater accuracy. (For more on making the jig, see "Making a Simple Box Joint Jig" on p. 42.) Setting up the box-joint jig to cut perfectly fitted joints can take some time, so keep scrapwood on hand to cut a sample joint or two. You will know that you are set up correctly when you can join two pieces together

WORK SMART

Whenever using a jig at the tablesaw, keep your body weight and slight pressure focused in a consistent direction. Leaning slightly in a uniform direction throughout a cut or process will overcome small inaccuracies or flex in the jig you're using.

without force, then hold one end of the assembly without gravity pulling the joint apart.

1. Begin cutting the joinery by setting the blade height slightly greater than the thickness of the box sides. Making the blade slightly higher will leave just a small amount of extra finger exposed to sand even with the box sides after assembly. Hold the pieces, long sides vertically, one at a time against the face of the box-joint jig. Align the bottom edge against the guide pin and make the first cut. Follow with each successive cut by lifting the stock up and over the guide pin. It is easy to get carried away and make too many cuts in this operation. Please note on the drawing on p. 39 to stop your cuts before you reach the top of the box. Keep your body weight slightly balanced to the right during the cut and also as the stock is pulled back from the blade. A smooth body motion will actually add to the accuracy of the fit of the part, particularly if there is any slop in the fit of the sled's runners in the tablesaw guide slots **(PHOTO A)**.

BEGIN CUTTING THE BOX JOINTS To cut the first finger of the box joint, butt the edge of the stock against the pin. For subsequent cuts, lift the fingers over the pin and lock the kerf in place on the pin. Note how the fingers stop shy of the top to leave room for the sliding lid.

B

CUT THE MATING PIECE Cutting finger joints in the mating parts requires you to make a cut in a piece of scrapwood, then place it in position over the guide pin. Butt the mating piece against the scrap and make one cut on each of the mating parts.

C

FINISH THE JOINT Step the stock over the guide pin for each cut until the part is complete. Be certain that the blade has passed all the way through the stock before repositioning.

2. Setting up to cut the mating parts on the jig requires the use of a piece of scrap stock. Hold the scrap against the guide pin and make a cut. This cut will form a single finger on the scrap stock. Adjust the fit of your scrap stock so that the single finger rests over the guide pin. In this position, the scrap will act as a spacer to control the position of the first cut on each mating piece **(PHOTO B)**.

3. After the mating parts have been cut, with a single finger formed on each, remove the scrap spacer and make the subsequent cuts. As you did on the long sides, make one cut, then lift the work-piece and fit the kerf you just cut over the guide pin. Proceed in this fashion until you've completed all the cuts **(PHOTO C)**.

MAKING A BOX-JOINT JIG

Despite the natural human inclination to over-complicate one's work, years of box making has taught me that simpler is usually better. I have used a variety of complex tablesaw jigs and confusing routing devices to cut box joints, but this straightforward jig sees a lot more use in my shop. Cutting box joints requires cutting a series of "fingers" such that the space between each finger is equal to the width of each finger. This jig makes it a simple process. It's also easy to make.

1. Drill a hole through the backing board for the guide pin. The hole should be drilled up from the edge of the stock to allow a little space for sawdust underneath, but low enough so that its height is less than the thickness of the stock used to make the box. Use a drill bit with a diameter equal to the width of the cut planned for the fingers of the joint. In this case, I use a ⅛-in. drill bit to match the ⅛-in. kerf of the combination blade I'll use to cut the joint. If you were using a ¼-in. dado set instead, you'd need to use a ¼-in. drill bit **(PHOTO A)**.

A

DRILL FOR THE GUIDE PIN Use a drill press and ⅛-in. bit to drill a hole for the guide pin. The hole should be inset from the edge of the jig but lower than the thickness of the wood you're joining.

2. I used a piece of ⅛-in. brass welding stock for the guide pin, but the broken-off shaft of an old ⅛-in. drill bit will work as well **(PHOTO B)**. Tap the guide pin in place and clamp the jig to the face of a miter guide or sled.

3. To use the jig, set the blade height just over the thickness of the stock and adjust the jig so that it is approximately ⅛ in. (the width of the sawblade) from the guide pin. Start with the stock firmly in place against the pin and make your first cut. Then lift the workpiece and position your cut over the guide pin to make your second cut. Continue making cuts along the width of the stock in this same manner. The round pin makes fitting the stock into place go quickly, and the small space under the pin prevents the occasional problem of sawdust getting in the way of the workpiece as you adjust for the next cut.

Run a test cut on scrap stock to allow for final adjustment **(PHOTO C)**. If the fingers fit too tightly, adjust the jig to narrow the space between the pin and the blade. If the fingers fit too loosely, widen the

B

INSERT THE GUIDE PIN
Use ⅛-in. brass rod to form the pin. For larger box joints, use a larger rod or the broken-off shaft of a drill or router bit.

space between the pin and the blade. You will know you have a perfect fit when the parts fit snugly together with only hand pressure. For help in trial-and-error adjustments see "Cut to Fit Using Trial and Error" on p. 46.

C

SET UP THE BOX-JOINT JIG
Use clamps to attach the box-joint jig to either a miter gauge or a tablesaw sled. It takes a bit of trial and error to get a perfect fit. Move the guide pin away from the blade to tighten the fit of the fingers. Move the pin toward the blade to loosen the fit.

Rout a groove to house the bottom

ONE OF THE CHALLENGING PARTS OF MAKING a box assembled with box joints is grooving the sides to fit the bottom without accidentally removing one of the fingers on the box joint. Instead of cutting a groove all the way to the end of the stock, I rout a stopped groove that won't interfere with the joinery. To cut this stopped groove, I use the router table outfitted with a fence and stop blocks, which limit the travel of the box parts in relation to the bit **(PHOTO A)**.

1. At the router table, use a ⅛-in. straight-cut bit raised ⅛ in. above the top of the table. For maximum cutting strength, I use a solid carbide bit with a single flute. Set each stop block so that the distance between the outside edge of the bit and the stop block is ¼ in. less that the length of the stock. This will control the length of travel so that the bit doesn't exit through the end of the stock. Use C-clamps to secure the stop blocks in place.

2. Begin by cutting the grooves in the long sides. Because the small fingers are fragile, this can be a delicate operation. To precut the portion of the groove most vulnerable to tearout, I use a simple process of lowering the stock onto the router bit at each extreme of the travel between the stop blocks (see the drawing below). In essence, you are merely drilling start and stop points at the extremes of router travel. When first performing this operation, you may find it helpful to turn the router off between steps.

3. Once the ends have been precut, rout the grooves by lowering the stock onto the bit and then guiding the stock along the fence between the stop blocks. It is important to maintain even pressure against the fence throughout the cut. When you have routed to the point where your stock abuts the other stop block, carefully raise the stock out of the cut.

4. To rout the grooves in the short sides, change the location of the stop blocks, then follow the procedure in step 2.

Rout blind slots

To reduce the risk of breaking the fingers off of the box-jointed sides, predrill the end of the grooves by registering one end of the stock against a stop block and lowering the other end onto the bit. Raise the stock off the bit and then repeat the process on the other end of the stock. To cut the grooves on the sides, lower the stock onto the bit and guide it along the fence between the stop blocks.

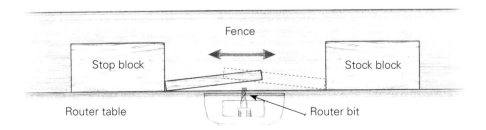

Move stock from right to left along fence

Fence

Stop block

Stock block

Router table

Router bit

A

ROUT A GROOVE FOR THE BOTTOM Stop blocks attached to the router table's fence allow you to cut stopped grooves on the sides. Without stop blocks, the grooves would be exposed on the finished box.

WORK
SMART

In our heads we can imagine how a certain operation is done, but in order to do it smoothly and safely our bodies need to learn the movements. When attempting a new task, practice the movements with the power off. Then turn on the tool and do it for real.

Make the bottom panel

TO SHAPE THE BOTTOM PANEL THAT RESTS in the grooves on the sides, use a tablesaw outfitted with a ¼-in. dado blade. Because the bottom of this box is made from hardwood, which shrinks and swells with seasonal changes in humidity, the bottom should be sized to accommodate movement. Allow about ¹⁄₃₂ in. expansion space when cutting the bottom to size.

1. Cut the ¼-in.-thick bottom to size at the tablesaw. Rip the stock to length first and then use the sled or a miter gauge to cut it to length.

2. Install a ¼-in. dado blade on your tablesaw and raise the blade to ⅛ in. A dial caliper will be useful in setting the blade height. Set the fence so that there is a ⅛-in. space between it and the inside edge of the dado blade.

3. Your finished tongue should be about ⅛ in. by ⅛ in., but it's a good idea to practice this cut on scrapwood and test the fit of the tongue in the actual box sides. With the stock held vertically against the fence, guide the stock across the blade. I interlock my hands over the top side of the fence so that I'm certain there is no danger of slipping into the blade. You may find it helpful to use a push stick to guide this cut.

4. Once you're ready to cut the rabbets on the actual bottom, cut the ends first so that any tearout that occurs will be removed as the sides are cut **(PHOTO A)**.

RABBET THE BOTTOM TO FIT THE GROOVE
Holding the stock upright against the fence, cut a small rabbet on the underside of the bottom. Rabbet the end grain first so that any tearout where the blade exits the cut will be removed when you cut the sides.

CUT TO FIT USING TRIAL AND ERROR

Adjusting tool settings to achieve a perfect fit can be a source of extreme frustration. In box making, measuring out exact sizes can be frustrating as well. Instead of relying totally on measurements, I have learned to cut things to fit. Knowing a precise method for making trial-and-error adjustments is the key to attaining a perfect fit. The result is much more exact that you could ever achieve using measurements alone.

If you try to change the location of a stop block by loosening the clamp and moving the stop block, the movement is almost always imprecise—you wind up moving it several times, checking the cut each time, and still getting no closer to the perfect fit. The secret I discovered is a two-handed sequence of changing stop-block locations.

To cut a piece slightly shorter, move the workpiece that amount away from the stop block with your right hand. Loosen the clamp securing the stop block and while holding the workpiece firmly in place move the stop block to touch the workpiece in its new position. Then retighten the clamp holding the stop block in place. To lengthen the cut, the sequence is slightly different. Hold the workpiece firmly in place while loosening the clamp holding the stop block in place. While still holding the workpiece tightly in position, move the stop block slightly away from the workpiece. The space opened between the workpiece and stop block should equal the amount of length you plan to add to the length of the stock. Retighten the stop block in its new position and proceed with your cuts.

Using this method of trial and error, the amount of change in one direction or the other can be accurately observed and controlled, making your adjustments to length of stock far more accurate than can be accomplished using the most accurate measuring tools.

TRIAL AND ERROR To shorten a cut, move the workpiece slightly away from the stop block and hold it firmly in place. Loosen the clamp and slide the stop block against the workpiece, then retighten the clamp. To lengthen a cut, move the stop block away from the workpiece.

Groove the sides to accommodate the top

THE SLIDING TOP OF THIS BOX IS BASED on the concept of the tongue-and-groove joint. A tongue formed on the sides of the lid allows it to slide within the grooves cut into the box sides. Because it requires no fitting of hardware and all the cuts can be made at the tablesaw, this is one of the easiest ways to add a lid to a box.

To cut the grooves in the sides, I use a ⅛-in.-kerf combination blade that has square teeth (instead of raked ones) because it allows you to cut flat-bottomed grooves in the sides.

1. Raise the blade ⅛ in. above the table height, then set the fence ⅜ in. from the outside edge of the blade. This allows you to cut the lid from ⅜-in. stock, then sand just a bit of the sides flush to the lid during final shaping.

2. Use a push block to guide the box sides through the cut. On cuts like this—where the saw teeth are buried beneath the face of the wood—the stock has a tendency to lift off the blade and leave shallow spots in the groove. Using a push block helps keep the stock flat to the table throughout the cut (**PHOTO** ).

It is easier to sand the interior of small boxes before they have been assembled. The outside surfaces can be sanded once assembly is complete.

A

CUT THE SIDES FOR THE LID TO FIT Use the tablesaw with a ⅛-in.-kerf combination blade to groove the box sides to accept the lid. Use a push stick to hold the stock securely throughout the cut.

3. After the slots are cut in the sides, raise the blade and trim the height of the box ends to allow clearance for the lid to slide open. To determine the fence location, measure from the bottom of the box sides to the edge of the groove cut for the sliding lid, then subtract $1/32$ in. for extra clearance. Because this stock is so small, use a push stick to guide the ends through the cut (**PHOTO B**).

TRIM THE HEIGHT OF THE ENDS To allow the lid to side freely across the ends of the box, cut away the top of the box ends. Take your measurement for this step directly from the height of the groove cut on the box sides.

Assemble the box

IF YOU ATTAINED A GOOD FIT IN CUTTING the joints, the box should go together smoothly without requiring any clamps. Very little glue is required to lock the joints in place and secure them for years to come.

1. Use a small squeeze bottle to apply glue to one set of fingers. As the joint is pushed together, the glue will spread and secure the joint. Attach the two short ends to one of the long sides, then slide the bottom into place and attach the last side (**PHOTO A**).

2. Make certain that the box is square before the glue dries. Either measure corner to corner and make adjustments until the two measures are identical, or check to see that the bottom panel fits evenly on all sides. In assembling this box, no glue should be applied to the bottom panel, leaving it free to expand and contract as humidity changes.

3. If the parts fit together tightly, there is no need to add clamps. If the fit is a little loose, use rubber bands, tape, or clamps to hold the corners in position until the glue sets.

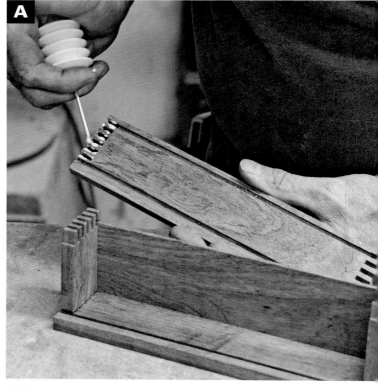

ASSEMBLE THE BOX Apply glue to the fingers using a squeeze bottle. Start with one side, add two ends and the bottom, then the other long side. No glue is required to secure the bottom. If the joints are well-fitted, no clamps are needed.

Fit and shape the lid

MAKING A LID THAT SLIDES SMOOTHLY IN the grooves requires a bit of trial and error. In fitting the lid, the feel of the lid moving in the grooves is more important than exact measured tolerances. Be prepared with a bit of scrapwood to test and fine tune your cut before you rabbet the actual lid to fit in the channels on the box sides.

1. Rip and crosscut the lid to size at the tablesaw.

2. A scrap remaining from cutting the lid to length is ideal for making a test cut. As you did to make the bottom panel, install a ¼-in. dado blade in the tablesaw. Raise the blade ⅛ in. above the saw table and position the fence so that the space between the blade and the fence equals the width of the grooves in the sides. To form the tongue on the lid, hold the lid on edge and firmly against the fence, then pass the stock across the blade **(PHOTO A)**. To prevent a loose-fitting lid, start with a saw setting that you know will be a bit too tight, then adjust the fence gradually until the lid slides smoothly in the grooves. Once you're satisfied with the fit of your test stock, make the same cuts in the lid.

3. The ends of the lid can be shaped to just about any pattern you like. To cut angled ends, use the tablesaw and a miter gauge **(PHOTO B)**. (A line marking the center of the lid helps in centering the cut, and a small line on the zero-clearance insert shows the exact cut line of the blade.) For a round shape, use a scrollsaw. I traced the base of a can to mark the round shape, but nearly any round object or a drafting compass would work as well **(PHOTO C)**.

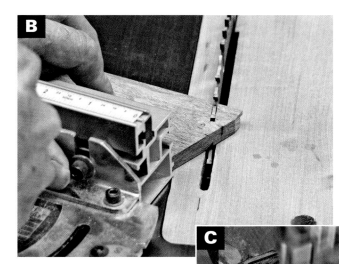

ONE WAY TO SHAPE THE LID Use the tablesaw and a miter gauge set at 15 degrees to shape the ends of the lid. Marks at the center of the stock and on the tablesaw insert are used to align the cuts.

CUT THE LID TO FIT Rabbet the lid to fit the grooves in the long sides. Trial and error may be required to obtain a perfect fit.

ANOTHER OPTION FOR THE LID To round the ends of the lid, use a scrollsaw. Any round object can be used as a template to mark out the shape.

4. As a final step in shaping the lid, use a small chisel to trim the tongue even with the box sides. To avoid damaging the finished lid, remove bits of the tongue in very small slices (**PHOTO D**).

TRIM THE CORNERS OF THE LID Use a chisel to trim the exposed tongues of the lid to align with the edges of the box in the closed position. Trimming the tongues is an optional step that makes the box slightly more atractive in the closed position.

Install the lid stop

THE LID STOP CONSISTS OF A ⅛-IN.-DIA. brass pin that passes through the lid. Once installed, the pin limits the travel of the lid, keeping it from coming out of the grooves completely. As its name implies, the lid stop also provides a clear stopping point when the lid is closed.

1. Slide the lid into the box to the closed position, then make a pencil line on the underside of the lid to record its location in the closed position (**PHOTO A**).

2. Measuring from your line toward the middle of the lid, mark out the thickness of the box end plus one-half the thickness of the dowel used as a stop. For this lid, the sides are ⅜ in. and the pin is ⅛ in. dia., so I measured ⁷⁄₁₆ in. from my pencil line and marked the lid for drilling.

3. Use a drill press to drill for the lid stop. A hand drill could be used for this operation—just be sure to hold the drill square to the stock as you drill (**PHOTO B**).

4. Use a hacksaw to cut the brass stock to length. Sand the edges of the pin by rolling the stock against a piece of sandpaper. Completely sand and finish your box and lid prior to installing the pin. When the oil finish is dry, slide the lid in place to a partially open position, then push the pin in place. Some light tapping may be required.

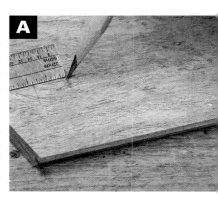

MARK FOR THE LID STOP To locate the end stop, mark out the position of the end while the box is in the closed position. Measure in from that mark to accommodate the thickness of the end stock as well as half the thickness of the pin.

> After finishing, use a bit of paste wax on the edges and tracks of sliding lids to help them move smoothly in the grooves.

DRILL FOR THE STOP PIN The lid's stop pin is housed in a hole drilled into the top. Use a ⅛-in. bit at the drill press and drill all the way through the lid. If you use a hand drill instead, be sure to keep the bit square to the lid.

**Change the look of your box drastically by
using different techniques or other species of wood.**

ASIDE FROM USING A DIFFERENT SPECIES OF
wood or using a combination of woods—walnut for the
box and spalted pecan for the lid, for instance—a few
simple techniques can change the character of this box
dramatically. One variation I like is to build this same
box with angled sides, lending the box a sculptural look.
Another option is to use a lift lid, similar to the one found
on the lift-lid box on p. 4, but fitted with a pull.

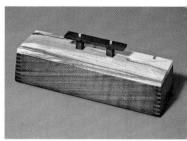

BEVEL BOTH SIDES To create a box with
beveled sides, thicker stock should be used. Once
the box is assembled, angle the blade and trim
the sides. For the safety of your hands, keep them
wrapped over the fence throughout the cut.

ANGLED SIDES To create a box with angled
sides, you'll need to build the box with thicker
stock. The thicker stock will allow you to trim
away part of the sides without sacrificing
strength at the groove where the sliding lid fits.
I use 7/16-in. stock for the sides of angled boxes.

1. Once the box is assembled, tilt the tablesaw
arbor to 5 degrees, then adjust the fence so that
the blade clears the side of the box at the top of
the cut **(PHOTO A)**.

2. To shape the ends of the box, use the miter
gauge on the tablesaw to guide the box through
the blade **(PHOTO B)**.

BEVEL THE ENDS
Trim the ends of
the box to the same
angle using your
miter gauge. A stop
block clamped to the
miter gauge can be
used to help position
the cut.

LIFT LID WITH A SIMPLE PULL This basic design can be modified to accept a lift lid rather than the sliding top, allowing the box to serve as a gift or presenation box. You'll need to cut the box joints all the way to the top of the sides (instead of stopping short to allow for

ASSEMBLE THE PULL Use cyanoacrylate glue to hold the parts together temporarily. Dowels are then used to secure it to the lid and reinforce the joint.

SHAPE THE LID Give additional interest to the lid of the box by shaping it with the tablesaw. Here, the ends of the lid are beveled at the tablesaw.

2. Use cyanoacrylate glue to hold the parts together before installing them on the box lid. Although some craftsmen have noted failure over time of cyanoacrylate-glued joints, the glue used here only needs to hold long enough for dowels to reinforce the joints **(PHOTO B)**.

3. Carefully mark the location of the pull on the lid. Using cyanoacrylate glue, you won't get much chance to adjust things.

4. Using a drill bit of the same diameter as your dowels, drill through the lid and into the pull **(PHOTO C)**.

5. Put a drop of glue in the hole and then tap the dowel in place.

the sliding top). Once the box has been assembled, make the lift lid following the same procedures used to make the lift-lid box on pp. 19–20. You can give the lid and base a more interesting shape by following the steps in making the angle-sided variation, then shaping the lid with the arbor tilted 10 degrees on the tablesaw **(PHOTO A)**.

A shopmade pull is another detail I often add. The pull seen here is made using two pieces of walnut stock $5/16$ in. by $7/16$ in. by $5/8$ in. long glued to a $1/8$ in. by $5/8$ in. by $3\frac{1}{2}$ in. long walnut top. Use $1/8$-in.-dia. dowels to attach the pull permanently.

1. Cut stock to size using your tablesaw and a crosscut sled. Use a stop block to control the length of cut and the eraser end of a pencil to hold the small parts in place.

ATTACH THE PULL WITH DOWELS Use the drill press to drill through the pull and into the lid. The dowels can be sanded flush or left slightly proud of the pull.

A Stationery Box with Hidden Splines

MADE OF ASH AND walnut, this box is designed to hold stationery, envelopes, stamps, and a pencil or two. It can be made with or without the simple tray, and it can be modified slightly in size and depth to fulfill any number of uses. Unlike the previous box that used visible keys to strengthen the miter joints, the corners of this box gain strength from hidden splines that are unseen from the outside of the box. This method allows the undisturbed beauty of the wood to be the strongest feature.

The overlapping raised panel lid is cut away from the base after the box is assembled and the glue has cured. Cutting the lid from the base after assembly guarantees that the lid and base are in perfect alignment, and that the grain an exact match. The lift lid on this box features a handle made from walnut, which contrasts nicely with the ash used for the sides. This unique handle can be used to either lift the lid from the base or to lift and move the whole box.

Hidden-spline stationery box

Built of ash and walnut, this stationery box features hidden-spine corners that provide significant strength without disturbing the beautiful grain at the corners of the box.

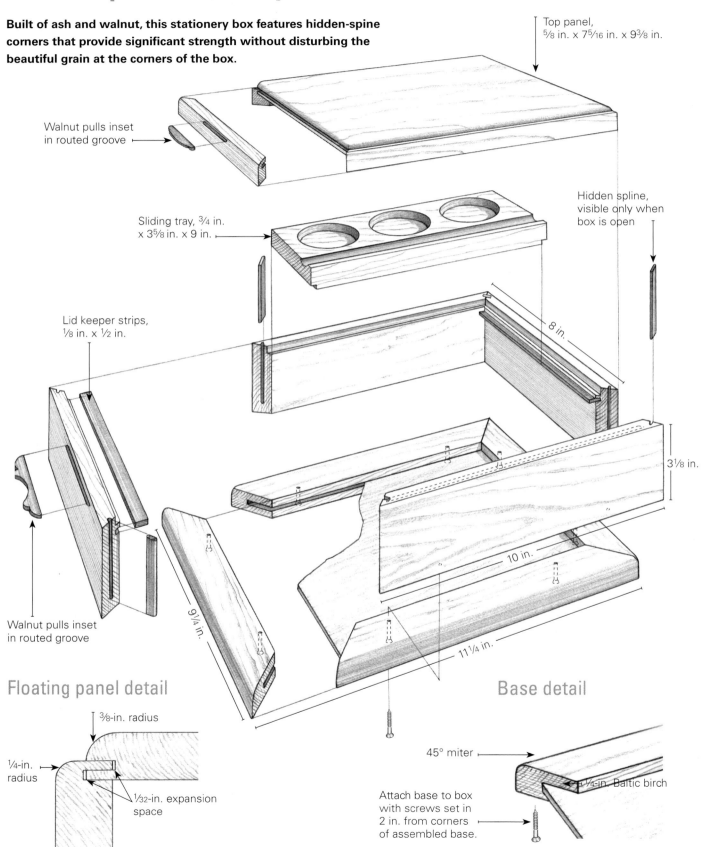

Top panel,
⅝ in. x 7⁵⁄₁₆ in. x 9⅜ in.

Walnut pulls inset in routed groove

Hidden spline, visible only when box is open

Sliding tray, ¾ in. x 3⅝ in. x 9 in.

8 in.

Lid keeper strips, ⅛ in. x ½ in.

3⅛ in.

10 in.

9¼ in.

11¼ in.

Walnut pulls inset in routed groove

Floating panel detail

⅜-in. radius

¼-in. radius

¹⁄₃₂-in. expansion space

Base detail

45° miter

¼-in. Baltic birch

Attach base to box with screws set in 2 in. from corners of assembled base.

QUANTITY	PART	ACTUAL SIZE	CONSTRUCTION NOTES
2	Ends	½ in. x 3¼ in. x 8 in.	Ash, size allows for saw kerf separating lid from base
2	Front and back	½ in. x 3¼ in. x 10 in.	Ash, size allows for saw kerf separating lid from base
1	Floating top panel	⅝ in. x 7⁵⁄₁₆ in. x 9⅜ in.	Ash, size allows for ¹⁄₁₆ in. expansion in width
1	Bottom	8 ¼ in. x 10¼ in.	¼-in. Baltic birch plywood
2	Base ends	¾ in. x 1¼ in. x 9¼ in.	Ash
2	Base front and back	¾ in. x 1¼ in. x 11¼ in.	Ash
2	Lid keeper strips	⅛ in. x ⁷⁄₁₆ in. x 7¼ in.	Walnut, mitered to fit recess in box sides
2	Lid keeper strips	⅛ in. x ⁷⁄₁₆ in. x 9¼ in.	Walnut, mitered to fit recess in box front and back
2	Tray supports	⅛ in. x ⁷⁄₁₆ in. x 7 in.	Walnut
1	Tray	¾ in. x 3⅝ in. x 9 in.	Ash
4	Splines	³⁄₁₆ in. x 2⅝ in. x ⅜ in. stock	Cut from ³⁄₁₆-in. x 2⅝-in.
4	Pulls	⅛ in. x ⅝ in. x 2½ in.	Walnut, cut and shaped to fit in ⅛-in. x 2½-in. slots in box lid and sides

Prepare the stock

TO DETERMINE THE AMOUNT OF MATERIAL required to make this box, add the lengths of both sides and both ends, then add at least 1 in. extra to allow a small amount of waste in cutting the parts to length. To thickness the stock to its final ½-in. dimension, you can either resaw the stock on the tablesaw or run it through the thickness planer. Before mitering the ends of the stock, rip the length of stock to final width at the tablesaw.

Always using the same blade with your tablesaw sleds makes marking out cuts simple. Mark the cut line in pencil on the stock and then align the pencil line with the cut line on the sled's fence.

Two different types of miter sleds are used to build both this box and the variations shown in the "Design Options" on p. 78. The first miter sled is used to cut wide stock and is designed for use with the blade tilted to 45 degrees. The second is a more common miter sled often used by craftsmen in cutting picture-frame parts. You'll use it to cut trim and frame parts, and it may turn out to be the most useful tablesaw accessory in your shop. Both of these sleds offer greater safety and accuracy than a standard tablesaw miter gauge.

MITER SLED FOR WIDE STOCK

The wide-stock miter sled on the facing page is a smaller version of the crosscut sled many cabinet-makers use. This design is scaled to a size useful in box making, and unlike most sleds this one takes up little storage space when not in use. The sled's reduced weight also allows it to move through cuts with less resistance. To make this sled, follow the steps shown in "Making a Crosscut Sled" on p. 28, then add wood stock to the front and back of the sled as shown.

ATTACH FRONT AND BACK
Align the front and back fences with the edges of the plywood base, then countersink screws to attach them in place.

MAKE YOUR FIRST CUT
An exact first cut allows you to measure from that mark whenever you're using the sled. Also, you can use the sled to help set the blade angle later. Rotate the blade (by hand) through the kerf in the sled. If the blade scrapes at all, the angle of the blade should be adjusted.

Wide-stock miter sled

Used with the blade angled to 45 degrees, this tablesaw sled allows you to cut accurate miters. Used with a stop block clamped to the fence, you can cut multiple mitered pieces to exactly the same length.

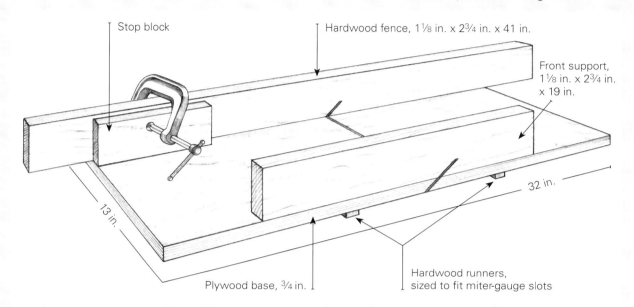

Stop block

Hardwood fence, 1⅛ in. x 2¾ in. x 41 in.

Front support, 1⅛ in. x 2¾ in. x 19 in.

32 in.

13 in.

Plywood base, ¾ in.

Hardwood runners, sized to fit miter-gauge slots

WIDE MITER SLED MATERIALS

QUANTITY	PART	ACTUAL SIZE*	CONSTRUCTION NOTES
1	Base	¾ in. x 13 in. x 32 in.*	Plywood or MDF
2	Runners	⅜ in. x ¾ in. x 13 in.	Hardwood, sized to fit tablesaw guide slots
1	Fence	1⅛ in. x 2¾ in. x 41 in.	Hardwood
1	Front support	1⅛ in. x 2¾ in. x 19 in.	Hardwood
14	Screws	#6 drywall, 1¼ in.	

*These dimensions are not critical to the success of the sled.

LOW MITER SLED

The low miter sled seen on p. 58 has been in regular use in my shop for many years—proof that this simple sled is well worth the time it takes to make it. Used with the blade at 90 degrees, this sled works well for mitering low stock, making custom trim, cutting miter keys, and much more. As with other tablesaw sleds, stop blocks can be clamped to the fence to improve accuracy and cut parts that match exactly.

continued ▶ ▶ ▶

To make this sled, begin by using the same method used to build the crosscut sled shown p. 28. When the runners are attached, place the sled on the tablesaw and mark the blade location, then use a square and pencil to extend the line of the tablesaw cut. Instead of adding a 90-degree fence, as is used with a crosscut sled, cut a 45-degree piece from a corner of scrap plywood or MDF. Use a combination square to position the plywood over the mark where the saw will cut, then screw the corner into place. Take care to see that the screws aren't placed in the path of the blade. If you don't glue this piece in place, you'll be able to disassemble it for future repairs. Cut two pieces of hardwood to act as fences, miter one end of each, then screw them in place so that their sides abut the plywood or MDF center piece. You'll use these strips to attach stop blocks with C-clamps for cutting multiple parts to the same size.

Miter sled for low stock

Used with the blade at 90 degrees, this small sled excels at mitering thin or low stock, and will provide for quick miter cuts with very little set-up time.

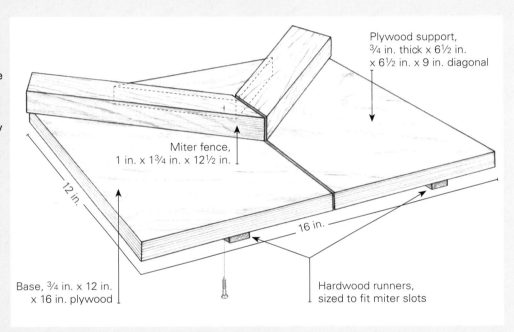

Plywood support, ¾ in. thick x 6½ in. x 6½ in. x 9 in. diagonal

Miter fence, 1 in. x 1¾ in. x 12½ in.

12 in.

16 in.

Base, ¾ in. x 12 in. x 16 in. plywood

Hardwood runners, sized to fit miter slots

LOW MITER SLED MATERIALS

QUANTITY	PART	ACTUAL SIZE	*CONSTRUCTION NOTES
1	Base	¾ in. x 12 in. x 16 in.*	Plywood or MDF
2	Runners	⅜ in. x ¾ in. x 12 in.	Hardwood, sized to fit tablesaw guide slots
1	Backing	¾ in. x 6 in. x 6 in. x 8⅝ in.	90° triangle plywood or MDF
2	Fences	1 in. x 1¾ in. x 12½ in.	Hardwood
12	Screws	#6 drywall, 1¼ in.	

*These dimensions are not critical to the success of the sled.

Miter the corners

I MITER AND CUT THE STOCK TO FINAL
length in a single pass at the tablesaw. I angle the
blade to 45 degrees and use a miter sled with a stop
block to control the length of the cut. This same
operation can be done with a standard tablesaw
miter gauge, but I prefer the sled because it is safer
and more accurate. Before cutting miters on your
actual stock, tilt the blade to 45 degrees and make
a test cut on scrapwood. Check the accuracy of the
cut with a combination square. When you are satisfied with the accuracy of the cut, proceed in mitering the parts for the box front, back, and sides.

1. Crosscut the stock at the center, dividing it into
two pieces of equal length. From each of these two
lengths of stock you'll cut one side and one end. To
help align the stock against the sled's fence, I mark
the center of the stock and align it with the cut line
on the sled's fence.

To modify instructions from a left-tilt
saw for use on a right-tilt saw, follow
the same steps but place your stop
blocks on the left side of the fence
rather than the right. Trim one miter
with the face side down, flip the
stock over, and position it against the
stop block on the left to miter the
opposite end.

2. Make the first mitered cut on the box ends
with the blade angled to 45 degrees and the exterior face of the sides down on the base of the sled.
The object at this point is to form the miter on
one end of each piece **(PHOTO A)**.

A

**MITER ONE
END OF THE
STOCK** Begin
cutting the
sides to length
by mitering the
first end of each
piece. Place the
stock face side
down on the
sled and make
the cut.

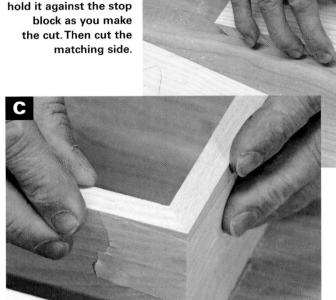

CUT THE SIDES TO LENGTH Flip the stock over so that the face side is up and hold it against the stop block as you make the cut. Then cut the matching side.

CHECK THE FIT OF THE MITER Taping the miters together on their outside faces is an easy way to check the fit of the miters.

3. Clamp your stop block in place on the sled's fence, then cut the front and back of the box to final length. Flip the stock over so that the outside face is turned up on the sled, then slide the already mitered end against the stop block and make the cut. **(PHOTO B).**

4. Adjust the location of the stop blocks to cut the two ends of the box. Once all four pieces are cut, you can test the accuracy of your miters by assembling the sides and ends with masking tape. **(PHOTO C).**

Fit the raised panel

THE TOP OF THIS BOX IS A FLOATING RAISED panel that rests in grooves cut into the box sides. Preparing the box for a floating panel lid requires making matching cuts on all four sides of the box and on each edge of the lid. This requires careful measuring and a few test cuts on scrap stock before you cut the actual sides or top. If you are like me, finding the perfect fit may require more than one test cut.

This particular type of floating panel is ideal for boxes because, unlike more conventional raised panels, the space required for expansion and contraction of the wood is completely hidden from view. Because the top overlaps the box sides, it adjusts to changes

in atmospheric humidity with no observable effects. The grooves in the box sides and the edges of the top panel are identical, each requiring the same blade and fence settings at the tablesaw. The cuts differ in that the box sides are cut face side up on the surface of the tablesaw and the panel is cut with the inside face flat against the surface of the tablesaw fence.

1. Plane the top panel to ⅝ in. thick and cut it to size at the tablesaw. The cutting list on p. 55 provides a general idea of the size, but small inaccuracies in cutting the box sides and ends may require you to adjust the size of the top.

SET UP TO GROOVE THE TOP PANEL AND SIDES To groove the top panel and sides, set up the fence so that there is ⅛ in. between it and the inside edge the blade. Test the cut by passing two pieces of scrapwood through the cut. A trial fitting should allow the two cuts to interlock.

CUT THE TOP AND SIDES TO FIT All four sides and the top panel are cut using the same settings on the saw. Cut the sides with the inside faces down against the tablesaw top. Then cut the top panel on edge with the inside face against the fence.

When forming floating panels, cut the end grain first so that any resulting tearout will be removed when the side grain is cut.

2. With a ⅛-in.-kerf sawblade installed in your tablesaw, raise the blade to cut ¼ in. deep. Adjust the space between the blade and the fence to equal the width of the saw kerf (⅛ in.). Before cutting the lid or sides, make test cuts on two pieces of scrap stock. This size of the stock is not important—just be sure you make one cut with the flat face against the saw fence and the other with the flat face down on the tablesaw top to represent the relationship between the sides and top panel of the box. Adjust the blade settings until the scrap top and scrap side go together easily but without any slop in the fit **(PHOTO A)**.

3. When you are satisfied with the fit of the scrap stock, make cuts along the top of each box side with the inside faces down against the top of the tablesaw.

4. To cut the top panel, hold it vertically against the fence as it crosses the blade. Cut the end grain first and then the side grain. When you cut in this order, any tearout in cutting end grain will be removed in the final cuts **(PHOTO B)**.

5. Test the fit of the panel in the box sides. If the fit is too snug, it can be adjusted by moving the fence very slightly toward the blade and recutting.

Cut the hidden-spline joinery

USING HIDDEN SPLINES TO BRIDGE THE COR-NER joints on this box enables you to strengthen the glue joints in a way that is completely unseen once the box goes together. Hidden splines are a great joinery choice when you are trying to highlight the grain of your primary wood and aiming for a design with simple lines. The splines are short lengths of wood that are set into slots cut in the mitered ends of the sides and ends. Because I wanted the ends of the splines to be unseen on the top and bottom of the box, I made a quick router jig to cut stopped grooves in the mitered ends of the stock (see "Hidden-Spline Jig" on p. 64. This simple jig holds the box side stock at 45 degrees as it passes over the router bit. By moving the jig along a fence and between stops on the router table, blind slots are easy to cut.

One of the challenges of this technique is keeping your body moving smoothly while leaning into the fence during the cut. When teaching beginning and even advanced box makers this technique, I ask them to practice the movement of the jig along the fence even before the router is turned on.

1. To determine the correct fence position, place the jig on the router table and adjust the fence so that there is a ⅛-in. space between the 45-degree angled surface of the jig and the inside edge of the bit.

BEGIN CUTTING THE SPLINE SLOT Begin cutting the hidden-spline slot by lowering the jig and workpiece into the cut. Start the cut with the jig held tightly against the stop block on the right side of the router table.

ALIGN THE SIDES ON THE HIDDEN-SPLINE JIG Use a flat surface to align each end of the box sides on the jig, then use a clamp to secure it in place. Lift the jig up after clamping and check by feel that the bottom edges are aligned.

2. To determine the position of the stop blocks, place a piece of mitered stock in the jig with the mitered side facing out. Measure and mark equal distances from each side of the stock to the proposed endpoints of the hidden spline. Hook the end of a tape measure on the left side of the stock and move the jig until the mark on the right side of the stock aligns with the right side of the router bit. Note the measurement on the tape and clamp the left stop block in place. Then hook the tape measure on the right side of the jig and slide it to the right until the distance measured to the left side of the router bit equals what you measured on the right. Hold the jig in position, slide the stop block against it, then clamp it in place.

3. Align the box side against the hardwood strip on the jig. To make sure the end of the mitered side is flush with the bottom of the jig, hold the box side and jig on a flat surface. When you feel the jig and box side both bottom out on the surface, clamp the side in place (**PHOTO A**).

4. Position the back of the jig against the fence and the right side of the jig against the stop block, then slowly lower the jig onto the spinning router bit. Guide the jig along the fence and toward the opposite stop block, then clear the tightly packed sawdust from the newly routed groove by returning the jig to its original position (**PHOTO B**). Most problems in using this technique come from failure to hold the jig firmly against the fence while routing the slots. Be sure to keep firm pressure on the jig against the fence throughout the cut (**PHOTO C**).

5. Repeat the same steps to rout slots in both ends of the sides and ends of the box. Once all the slots are cut, compare the finished cuts to make certain they are all uniform (**PHOTO D**).

FINISH CUTTING THE SPLINE SLOT Move the jig from right to left between stop blocks, then move the stock back to the right where you began the cut. Hold the jig tightly against the fence throughout the cut. Careful control keeps the stock from climbing away from the fence and widening the cut.

THE FINISHED SLOTS The finished slots should be inset from the ends of the stock $3/8$ in. and be about $3/16$ in. deep.

To avoid mistakes in cutting, take time to carefully arrange and mark your parts. In preparation for a series of cuts, orient each part with the same side up and the same edge toward the fence.

This jig is designed for the simple task of holding mitered stock at an exact 45-degree angle as it passes across the router table. The jig is used to move between stops as it cuts blind grooves for corner splines. It is quickly made by cutting a piece of 7½-in.-wide stock into two separate pieces using the wide miter sled seen on pp. 56–57. Once the parts are cut, flip one piece over and attach it using a nail gun and glue. It is important to hold the parts tightly in position as they are nailed. Add a mitered strip at the front edge to help hold the part in alignment during the routing operation.

NAIL THE JIG TOGETHER I use a pneumatic nailer to assemble the jig, but a hammer and nails will also work. If you're using a hammer and nails, tape the parts together while the glue dries. Then predrill the holes for screws or nails.

Hidden-spline router jig

Used with a straight bit in the router table, this jig enables you to rout blind channels on the mitered ends of stock. With the work clamped in place, the jig rides along the fence between stop blocks.

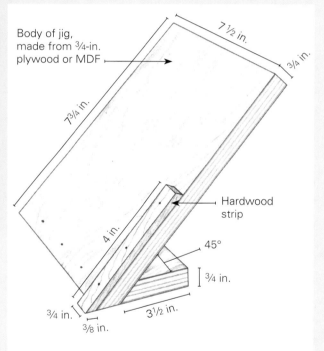

Body of jig, made from ¾-in. plywood or MDF

7 ½ in.

¾ in.

7¾ in.

4 in.

Hardwood strip

45°

¾ in.

¾ in.

3½ in.

⅜ in.

Assemble with glue and nails or screws

QUANTITY	PART	ACTUAL SIZE	CONSTRUCTION NOTES
1	Base	¾ in. x 7½ in. x 7¾ in.*	¾-in. plywood or MDF
1	Base	¾ in. x 3½ in. x 7½ in.*	¾-in. plywood or MDF
1	Alignment strip	⅜ in. x ¾ in. x 4 in.*	Hardwood

*45° angle cut at one end.

Make the splines

For maximum strength, the grain of the splines should run in roughly the same direction as the grain in the box sides. It's easiest to make all of the spline stock in one long strip and then cut each spline to the correct length. To determine the width of the spline stock, measure the width of the groove cut in the mitered ends of your box sides. To determine the length of the splines, measure the depth of one slot, double it, and subtract about 1/64 in. to allow for glue.

1. Plane material to the same thickness as the width of the slots. To avoid difficulty during assembly, be sure that the fit is not too tight. Inserting or removing the spline stock should require little effort because even greater force will be needed once the glue is

FIT THE SPLINES TO THE SLOTS Take light passes through the thickness planer until the spline stock fits snugly in the hidden-spline slot. The spline stock should fit easily into the slots and yet have enough resistance to hold against gravity.

SHAPE THE SPLINE STOCK Use a 1/16-in.-radius roundover bit to shape the edges of the spline stock. If you're only making a single box, it's often faster to sand the edges round with coarse sandpaper. Check the width of the spline stock so that it fits in the slots.

CUT THE SPLINES TO LENGTH Use a crosscut sled outfitted with a stop block to cut the splines to length. For safety, use the eraser end of a pencil to hold the small offcuts and remove them following the cut.

CHECK THE FIT OF THE SPLINES Once the splines are cut to size, they should slide easily into the slots on your box sides and the miters should close with the splines in place.

applied. It's a perfect fit when the spline material will stay in place when turned upside down but will fall out with just a bit of shaking **(PHOTO E)**.

2. After planing the material to thickness, cut it to width at the tablesaw.

3. Pass the length of spline stock across a 1/8-in. roundover bit in the router table. Rounding the edges of the splines helps achieve a perfect fit in the rounded grooves **(PHOTO F)**.

4. Cut the spline stock to length at the tablesaw using a crosscut sled with a stop block clamped in place. The sled allows the cut splines to be safely controlled during the cut and the stop block assures that they are cut to a uniform length **(PHOTO G)**.

5. To avoid any surprises during assembly, check the fit of all the splines prior to gluing up the box. The mitered joint should close completely with the spline in place **(PHOTO H)**.

Prepare the inside before assembly

ONCE FINISHED, THE INSIDE OF THE BOX is outfitted with a small organizing tray that rests on supports set into the sides of the box. It's easiest to go ahead and cut the joinery for the supports before assembling the box. You'll also want to rout dados on the inside of the box to house the lid keeper strips. As with any small box, sanding all the interior surfaces prior to assembly saves lots of hard work.

1. Dadoes are used to house the keeper strips that hold the lid in place. Use the router table to cut ¾-in.-wide dadoes in the inside faces of the sides and ends. Raise the cutter about ⅛ in. above the surface of the table and set the fence so that there is a ⅝-in. space between it and the inside edge of the cut **(PHOTO A)**.

2. At the tablesaw, cut grooves in the ends of the box to house the tray supports. Use a ⅛-in.-kerf blade set to cut ⅛-in.-deep grooves inset 1½ in. from the top edge of the box ends. Be careful to put the box front and back aside so you don't cut this groove in them by mistake **(PHOTO B)**.

3. To soften the exposed edges of the box, rout the sides and top panel using a ⅜-in.-radius roundover bit in the router table. Rout all four sides, as well as the top panel. Be sure the bit is raised high enough so that the full profile of the roundover is revealed and the edges of the cut are flush to the edge and side of the box. It's helpful to make a trial cut on scrapwood **(PHOTO C)**.

CUT THE RECESS FOR THE LIFT LID Use a ½-in. straight bit set ⅛ in. above the surface of the router table to rout each side with the inside face down and the top edges against the fence.

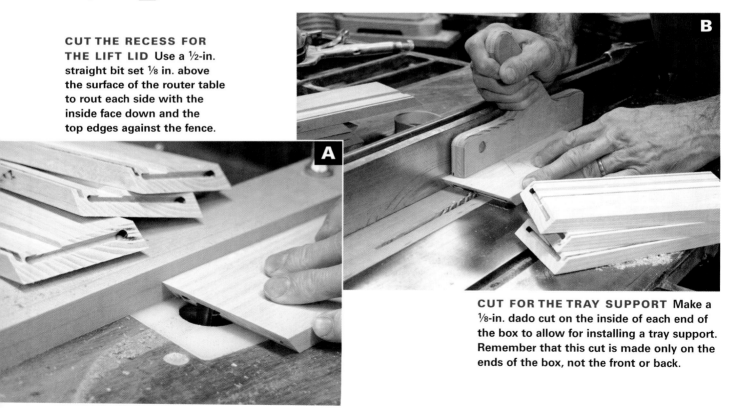

CUT FOR THE TRAY SUPPORT Make a ⅛-in. dado cut on the inside of each end of the box to allow for installing a tray support. Remember that this cut is made only on the ends of the box, not the front or back.

ROUT THE BOX EDGES AND TOP PANEL
Use a ⅜-in.-radius roundover bit in the router table to rout the top edges of the box sides and each edge of the top panel. Raise the height of the bit so that it cuts flush with the surface of the router table and set the fence so that it aligns with the flat face of the fence.

4. Just prior to assembly is the best time to sand the interior of the box and the inside of the top panel. I start with 180 grit paper and finish with 240 grit.

Glue up the box

Using a squeeze bottle helps you get in the spline slots and other tight spaces without making a mess of the box sides or any project parts.

ASSEMBLE THE BOX
Because mitered surfaces absorb glue quickly, coat each end of the mitered parts with glue.

WITH SMALL BOXES, IT'S EASY TO APPLY too much glue and make a mess of the assembly process. Using a squeeze glue bottle helps to apply a controlled amount of glue. Because you're gluing end grain to end grain, be sure to lay glue on both the mitered surfaces and in the grooves cut to house the splines. Using hidden splines makes the assembly process a little more involved. Using clamps helps

seat the splines firmly in the grooves and helps distribute the glue evenly.

1. Apply glue to mitered surfaces and to the interior of the grooves cut for the splines **(PHOTO A)**.

2. Use clamps to pull the joints tight at the corners. Make sure that the joints close up and check to

see that the box goes together square. To check for squareness, measure corner to corner from both directions and make sure that the measurements are the same. Alternately, use a carpenter's square set against the outside of the box. Often a simple squeeze across the long diagonal is enough to adjust the box to square (**PHOTO B**).

B

CLAMP IT UP Use of hidden splines requires clamping pressure to close up the miter joints. Check to be certain the assembly is square, then allow the clamps to hold things in place until the glue sets.

WORK
SMART

When assembling a box that requires clamps, get the clamps adjusted to approximate size before the glue is applied—it's an easy way to avoid needless fumbling and delays during assembly.

Cut the lid loose from the base

ON SMALL BOXES LIKE THIS, CUTTING THE lid from the base is easily done at the tablesaw after the glue has cured. The secret to cutting the top loose from the base is to lower the blade height so that the blade cuts almost through the stock but leaves a small sliver of wood to hold the lid and base together. The small sliver of wood keeps the base and lid in position so that the saw provides the cleanest and most accurate cut possible. It also prevents the pressure used to hold the box against the fence from pressing the offcut lid into the blade.

A

CUT THE LID FROM THE BOX Set the blade to cut a little shallower than the thickness of the box sides. When you pass the stock across the blade, a small sliver of wood will remain uncut.

1. Remember that the recess cuts that house the keeper strips reduce the necessary height of the blade. As a starting point, subtract ⅛ in. (the depth of the routed groove on the inside of the box) from the thickness of the box sides, then set your blade to that height. To check that the saw height is just right, use a razor knife to test your cut on the first side. The knife should push through the remaining wood with little effort. If the blade doesn't pierce the remaining wood with ease, raise the blade height slightly and try again. Once the blade is set to the correct height, cut the three remaining sides of the box **(PHOTO A)**.

2. Use a razor knife to separate the lid from the base. The knife should pass through the small thickness of stock easily. As the knife travels around the perimeter of the box, the lid will gradually fall away from the box **(PHOTO B)**.

CUT THE LID LOOSE WITH A KNIFE Use a knife to remove the small sliver of wood that remains uncut from the tablesaw. Cut all four sides with the knife, then lift the lid from the box.

Make and assemble the base frame

THE BOTTOM FRAME AND BALTIC BIRCH bottom panel for this box are a simple construction, with the Baltic birch plywood doing double duty. Fit into deep grooves cut into the inside edges of the frame, the bottom panel serves as both the bottom of the box and the joinery that secures the mitered corners of the base frame together. Because the plywood bottom is less prone to wood movement than hardwoods, you can safely glue the panel into the deep grooves cut on the base frame parts.

1. At the tablesaw, use a miter gauge or crosscut miter sled to cut the base frame parts to length.

Clamp a stop block in place to make certain that opposite sides of the frame come out the same length **(PHOTO A on p. 70)**.

2. To cut the groove for the Baltic birch panel, raise the blade of the tablesaw to 1 in. and pass each piece of base trim over the blade **(PHOTO B on p. 70)**.

3. Use a ⅛-in.-radius roundover bit in the router table to round the inside edges of the base trim. This operation must be done prior to assembly.

4. Sand the inside edges of all the base parts using 180 and then 240 grit paper.

MAKE THE BASE FRAME Use a miter gauge on the tablesaw to cut the base frame parts to size. A stop block is clamped in place on the miter gauge, assuring that the opposite sides are exactly the same length.

GROOVE THE FRAME Cut 1-in.-deep grooves on the inside edges of the frame to accept the plywood panel.

5. Apply glue to the mitered surfaces and into the corners of the grooves that house the plywood panel **(PHOTO C).**

6. Use a picture-framing clamp or band clamp to hold the assembly tight while the glue sets **(PHOTO D).**

7. Using the same router setting and bit you used to rout the box sides, profile the edges of the bottom assembly.

GLUE UP THE BASE Apply glue to both sides of the miters and into the grooves which house the plywood panel. The plywood panel serves as a bottom for the box and strengthens the miter joints on the base frame.

CLAMP THE BASE Adjustable band clamps and a very old picture-frame clamp are used to clamp the base parts together until the glue sets.

Add pulls to the box

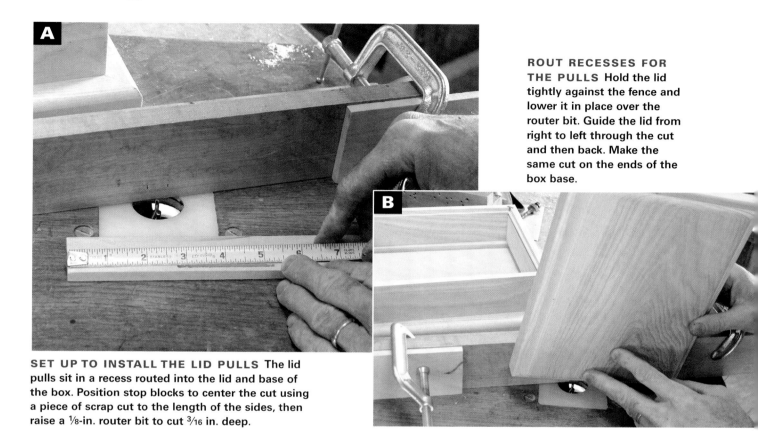

A

ROUT RECESSES FOR THE PULLS Hold the lid tightly against the fence and lower it in place over the router bit. Guide the lid from right to left through the cut and then back. Make the same cut on the ends of the box base.

B

SET UP TO INSTALL THE LID PULLS The lid pulls sit in a recess routed into the lid and base of the box. Position stop blocks to center the cut using a piece of scrap cut to the length of the sides, then raise a ⅛-in. router bit to cut ³⁄₁₆ in. deep.

THE SIMPLE WALNUT PULLS ON THIS BOX make it easy to lift the whole box as a unit or to lift only the lid. Using a router table and a ⅛-in. straight bit is the easiest way to rout the stopped channel that houses the pulls.

1. Measure the distance from the router bit to each stop block carefully. To achieve a pull of the length used in this box, the measurement from the far edge of the router bit to each stop block should be 5¼ in. Make a test cut on scrapwood cut to the same length as the ends of the box. Check the distance from each end of the stock to the routed channel and make sure each measurement is the same. If one measurement

is slightly different from the other, change the location of one stop block to center the cut **(PHOTO A)**.

2. Register the right side of the lid against the right stop block, then lower the lid onto the spinning blade. Pass the lid from right to left between the stop blocks, then from left to right as you return to starting position. If necessary, the channels can be widened slightly to fit thicker stock—just change the position of the fence and take another pass across the router bit **(PHOTO B)**.

3. Make the same cuts on the upper front edge on the box itself.

Cut and install the pulls

1. Use the tablesaw to cut the pull stock to thickness, then cut the pulls to length using a crosscut sled (**PHOTO C**).

2. Check the fit of the walnut stock in the routed channel. The stock should fit into place without excessive pressure (**PHOTO D**).

3. Use a roundover bit to round the ends of the pulls so that they fit the channels cut in the box ends. Clamping the pulls to a larger block allows

them to be routed safely. Flip them over to present different edges to the router bit (**PHOTO E**).

4. Fold cardstock to make a profile template for the front of your pulls. No exact shape is required, and scissors are all you need to cut it to shape. Note in **PHOTO F** that the design can be flipped to create a symmetrical shape at the opposite end. Mark one end of the stock using the template, then flip the template over to mark the opposite end.

CUT THE PULL STOCK TO LENGTH Use a tablesaw and crosscut sled to cut the lid pulls to length. Carefully check the fit against the routed slots in the lid and base.

FIT THE PULL TO THE LID Plane the stock for the pulls to the thickness of the recesses routed in the lid and base. A perfectly fitted pull should fit snug in the recess.

5. Use a scrollsaw to cut the pulls to shape **(PHOTO G)**.

6. Use sanding sticks wrapped in sandpaper to sand the pulls to their final shape.

7. Check the fit of the pulls prior to final assembly. They may require additional sanding to adjust their thickness **(PHOTO H)**.

ROUT THE PULLS Round the ends of the pulls using a ⅟₁₆-in. roundover bit. Clamping the pull stock to a wider piece of wood allows you to make this cut safely.

MAKE A TEMPLATE FOR THE PULLS Draw out and cut half of the profile of the pull on card stock. Position the template on one end of the pull stock and trace the pattern. Flip the template over and trace the pattern onto the other end of the pull.

CUT THE PULLS TO SHAPE A scrollsaw makes easy work of cutting the tight curves on the pulls.

INSTALL THE PULLS Once the pulls are smoothed, test their fit in the recesses on the box and lid. Only a few drops of glue are needed to secure them in place.

Install tray supports and lid keeper strips

A

CUT STRIPS FOR LID KEEPER STRIPS Cut ⅛-in.-thick walnut strips on the tablesaw. As you near the end of the cut, place a push block in place on the strip to guide it. A shopmade zero-clearance insert with integral splitter helps to control the cut.

THE WALNUT TRAY SUPPORTS FIT INTO THE grooves you cut earlier on the interior surfaces of the box ends. The lid keeper strips fit between the sides and the lid, holding it in position when the box is closed. Making the tray supports and keeper strips requires planing stock to its finished width and then cutting ⅛-in.-thick strips from it.

1. Plane the walnut stock you're using for the pulls to a thickness of ⁷⁄₁₆ in.

2. At the tablesaw, rip ⅛-in.-wide strips from the planed stock. As strips are cut, test their fit in the grooves and adjust the fence as required.

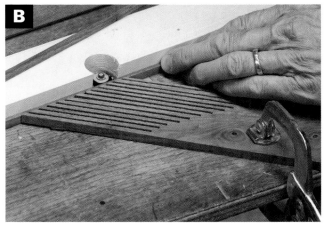

B

ROUT THE STRIPS A featherboard holds the strips tightly against the router fence as the edges are rounded with a ¹⁄₁₆-in. roundover bit.

I use a simple hold-down block to guide the strips through the cut and a shopmade zero-clearance insert and splitter to provide additional control. The hold-down in the left hand is pushed out of the way by the stop block at the end of the cut (**PHOTO A**).

3. Use the router table and a ¹⁄₁₆-in. roundover bit to profile the edges of the stock. Using a featherboard clamped to the router table allows you to keep your fingers out of the way as you rout the edges of the stock (**PHOTO B**).

4. Use a 45-degree cutoff sled on the tablesaw to cut the lid keeper strips to length. Clamp a stop block in place to control the length of cut (**PHOTO C**).

5. Cut the tray support stock to length and glue it in place in the grooves cut into the ends of the box (**PHOTO D**).

6. After installing the keeper strips, use a sanding block to sand the edges of the box. Sanding the edges of the keeper strips helps ease the fit of the lid as the box is closed.

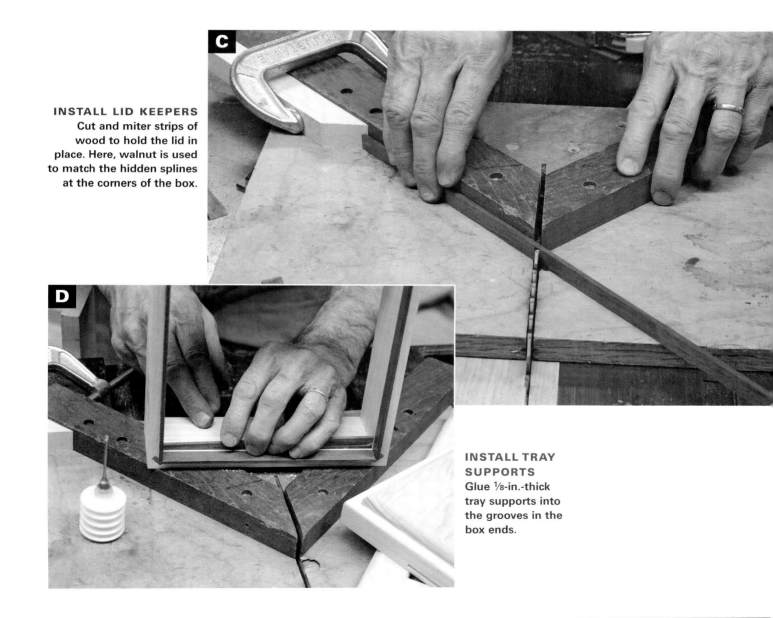

INSTALL LID KEEPERS
Cut and miter strips of wood to hold the lid in place. Here, walnut is used to match the hidden splines at the corners of the box.

INSTALL TRAY SUPPORTS
Glue ¹⁄₈-in.-thick tray supports into the grooves in the box ends.

Make the sliding tray

THE SLIDING TRAY INSIDE THIS BOX IS A nice surprise when you open the lid. The tray also provides a place to store stamps, paper clips, and other essential letter-writing accessories. In order to make a tray like the one seen in this box you'll need either a hole saw or adjustable circle cutter to form the template, a bowl routing bit to form the circular impressions, and a corebox bit to rout the pen slot.

1. Drill a 2³⁄₈-in. hole ¼ in. from the edge of ¾-in. scrap stock to serve as a routing template. Clamp the routing template in place so that it is aligned on one side of the stock you're using for the sliding tray. Use at least two clamps to keep the template from pivoting during the routing operation.

At this point, the stock for the tray should be cut to width but left long so that you have enough room to clamp your template in place. After routing one section, adjust the position of the template to rout two more sections with equal space between each **(PHOTO A)**.

2. Use the router table and a corebox bit to rout the groove for a pen or pencil to fit. Center the router cut to fit the remaining unrouted space in the tray **(PHOTO B)**.

3. Cut the tray to length to fit inside the box. If you'd like the tray to sit lower in the box, you can cut small rabbets on the underside at the ends of the tray.

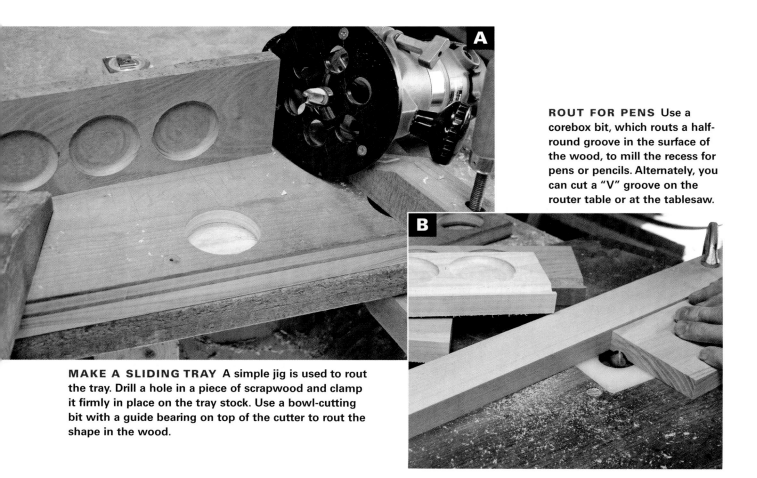

ROUT FOR PENS Use a corebox bit, which routs a half-round groove in the surface of the wood, to mill the recess for pens or pencils. Alternately, you can cut a "V" groove on the router table or at the tablesaw.

MAKE A SLIDING TRAY A simple jig is used to rout the tray. Drill a hole in a piece of scrapwood and clamp it firmly in place on the tray stock. Use a bowl-cutting bit with a guide bearing on top of the cutter to rout the shape in the wood.

Sanding, finishing, and final assembly

PREDRILL THE BASE Use the drill press outfitted with a fence to predrill screw holes through the base. Set the depth of the countersink so that the screw heads will fit just below the surface of the base.

SCREW BASE TO BOX SIDES Position the base on the box and clamp it in place. Drill through the holes in the base and into the box, then drive screws to secure the base.

SANDING AND FINISHING THE BOX PRIOR TO assembly provides easier access to all the surfaces and keeps the Danish oil from pooling in corners where it might be difficult to rub out.

1. Sand the sides, top, and base, starting with 180 grit paper and working through to 320 grit, then glue the pulls in place.

2. Apply the Danish oil finish in two or three coats, polishing with rags between each coat. Old cotton T-shirts are an excellent source of rags. Be sure to wipe any oil seeping out from the corners of miters, pulls, and trim. You may need to wipe down the finish more than once between coats.

3. After the finish has dried, attach the base to the sides of the box using screws driven from underneath. Predrilling through the holes in the base prevents breaking screws or splitting the sides of the finished box **(PHOTO A)**. Align the sides to the base by noting the intersection of the miters with the corners of the box, or by measuring in an equal distance from each side. Use clamps to secure the box sides to the base, then turn the box upside down to install the screws. Countersink the screws so that they are just slightly deeper than flush with the bottom of the base, then cover them with felt pads after assembly. Screws should not be placed exactly at the corners of the base where they might split or weaken the miter joints **(PHOTO B)**.

**Using highly figured woods can change the visual effect;
adding trim or carvings are two more difficult options
that produce stunning results.**

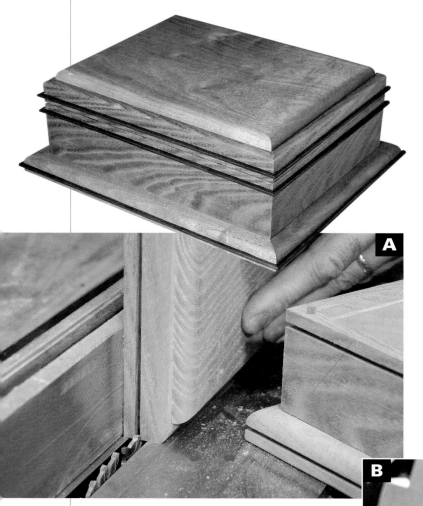

THIS BASIC BOX DESIGN OFFERS MANY

opportunities to make small design changes that
reflect your own tastes. Choose highly figured
woods or use keyed miters to give a more dramatic
visual effect. Two more challenging options are to
trim the box using a contrasting wood, as seen in
the box made of sassafras and walnut at left, or to
add a carved texture or design—both are good
ways to transform this straightforward design into
a real showpiece.

USE A CONTRASTING TRIM To add a contrasting trim, cut ⅛-in. strips of walnut when you
cut the lid keepers and tray supports. Be sure to cut
enough extra stock to allow for test cuts. You can also
rout the edges of the trim to add interesting details.
Any edge routing should be done prior to cutting
the stock to length. In the box seen at left, I used a
¹⁄₁₆-in.-radius roundover bit and followed the same
process used on p. 74. I prefer to cut the strips to fit
and then sand them prior to assembly. The sanding
helps to provide a little clearance so that the strips
can be glued in place more easily.

A

B

**CUT GROOVES FOR THE
TRIM STRIPS** Decorative
strips of a contrasting wood
are set into grooves cut around
the lid, box, and base. Cut the
grooves using a ⅛-in. combination blade set to cut ⅛ in. deep.

1. Cut the channels in the box sides and base using the tablesaw and a ⅛-in. combination blade raised to a height of ⅛ in. **(PHOTO A)**.

2. Use a miter sled outfitted with a stop block to cut the strips to length and miter their ends. This cut requires a little trial and error, so the extra stock comes in handy **(PHOTO B)**.

3. Working from corner to corner, glue the strips in place. Using a squeeze bottle of glue helps keep the glue inside the channel and prevents making a mess on the outside of the box **(PHOTO C)**.

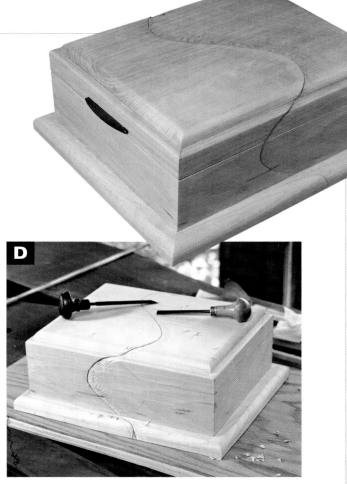

INSTALL THE TRIM STRIPS To install the strips, start at one corner of the box and work your way around the box.

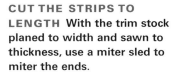

CUT THE STRIPS TO LENGTH With the trim stock planed to width and sawn to thickness, use a miter sled to miter the ends.

CARVE THE FINAL TOUCHES Simple carving tools are used to add interest to a rather plain box. This basswood box is carved using only a straight chisel and a shallow gouge.

ADD A CARVED TEXTURE Another option is to add interest by adding a carved texture. The box seen above was carved using only two simple tools: a straight chisel and a shallow gouge.

1. Use the straight chisel to form a meandering line across the edge of the base, up the sides, and across the top. Sketch a line in pencil first and begin cutting when you are pleased with the look **(PHOTO D)**.

2. Use the gouge to cut to a slight depth on one side of the line, which helps create the appearance of two separate planes.

3. Sand the carved areas and add simple lift tabs to the ends of the lid.

A Lap-Cornered Box

THE BOX SEEN HERE is built with quilted maple sides and a spalted maple lift lid. While making this box, you can choose your degree of involvement with handtools: The joints can be cut primarily with the tablesaw then simply cleaned up with a chisel, or you can go to the other extreme and cut the joints entirely by hand using a Japanese dozuki saw or backsaw. Either technique or a combination thereof can be used to build an attractive box and record your emergence as a true craftsman.

I particularly like boxes where the joinery is exposed so that you can tell exactly how the design is held together. With this design, even a quick glance at a distance allows the viewer to say, "I get it. ... I see how that works."

With this basic design, you can choose from an infinite range of variables to express your own creativity (see "Design Options" on p. 94).

A lap-cornered box

Cutting the exposed joinery on this lap-cornered design is a good way to hone and showcase your handtool skills. The box seen here features quilted maple sides and a spalted maple top.

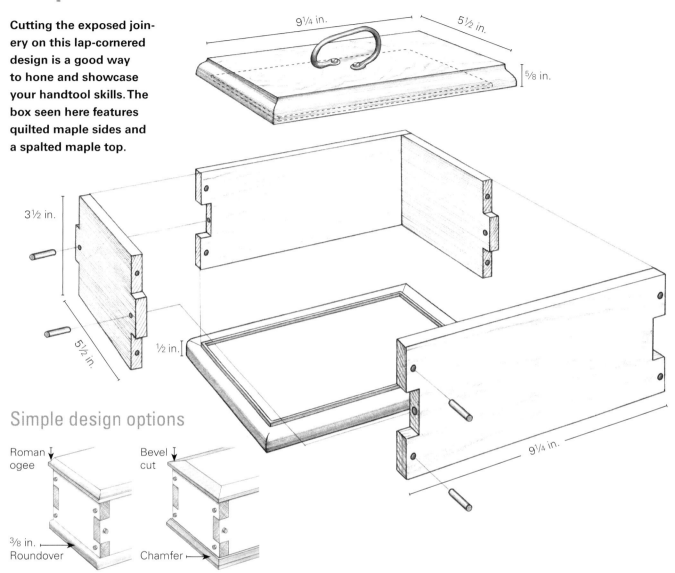

9¼ in.

5½ in.

⅝ in.

3½ in.

5½ in.

½ in.

9¼ in.

Simple design options

Roman ogee

Bevel cut

⅜ in. Roundover

Chamfer

MATERIALS

QUANTITY	PART	ACTUAL SIZE	CONSTRUCTION NOTES
2	Front and back	⅜ in. × 3½ in. × 5¹⁄₁₆ in.*	Quilted maple
2	Ends	⅜ in. × 3½ in. × 8¹³⁄₁₆ in.*	Quilted maple
1	Bottom	⅝ in. × 5½ in. × 9¼ in.	Quilted maple
1	Lid	¾ in. × 5½ in. × 9¼ in.	Spalted maple
1	Pull	2⅞-in. forged iron	Available from Horton Brasses, Inc. (stock number HF-20) www.hortonbrasses.com 800-754-9127

*Size includes ¹⁄₃₂-in. cleanup allowance at each end.

Begin with book-matched stock

PERFECTLY MATCHING GRAIN AT THE COR-
ners of a box can make the difference between a box that appears thoughtlessly put together and one that someone might consider art. There are two ways to get grain to match almost perfectly at the corners of a box. The first and most common method, which I've used earlier in this book, is to simply cut each piece in sequence from one long piece of stock. This technique gives you three perfectly matching corners and one that is often mismatched (where one end of the board meets the other).

Resawing and book-matching the parts, as shown in the drawing on the facing page, is an even better way to make sure that the grain flows perfectly around the corners of a box. Unlike the method using one long piece of wood, using book-matched stock creates a near perfect match at all four corners. Once you understand the process, it's pretty straightforward.

1. Resaw 1-in.-thick stock right down the middle so that the stock is divided into two pieces of equal thickness.

2. Plane each piece of resawn material to the finished thickness of the box sides.

3. Joint the edges of each piece and rip them to the final width at the tablesaw.

4. Stack the stock back in its original order and cut a section from one end long enough to form the front (or back) and one end.

WORK SMART

To maintain a close match between book-matched halves, do most of your thicknessing of stock from the face that will become the interior of the box.

A

MARK THE STOCK
Mark the two book-matched pieces of stock to denote front, back, left, and right. In addition, use an arrow to indicate the top edge of each part.

Two kinds of book-matching are useful in boxmaking

Resawing stock offers the opportunity to obtain two types of book-match, each useful in making boxes. A standard match is easier to understand. Looking at it from the end of the stock, you can see where it gets its name. The wood opens like a book. The end-to-end match allows for continuous grain around the corners of a box. It's much easier to understand when you try it yourself.

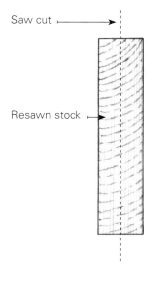

Saw cut

Resawn stock

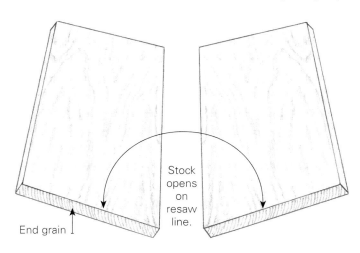

Standard book-match aligns side to side and is used when book-matching panels.

Stock opens on resaw line.

End grain

End-to-end book-matching sides for boxes

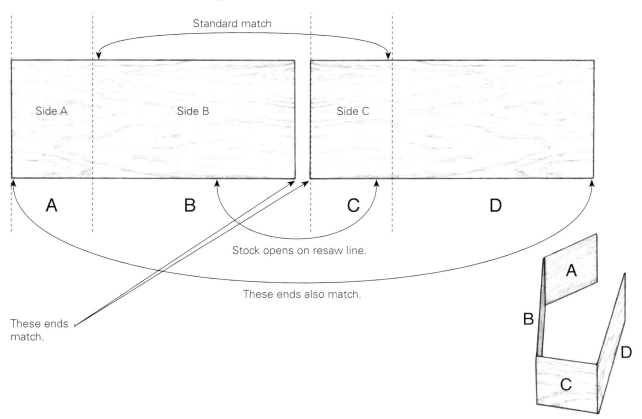

Standard match

Side A   Side B   Side C

A   B   C   D

Stock opens on resaw line.

These ends also match.

These ends match.

CUT THE FRONT, BACK, AND SIDES Use the sled on the tablesaw to cut the box ends to length. A stop block clamped to the fence guarantees that both pieces are the same length. Adjust the stop block to cut the front and back to exact length.

5. Mark each piece before the individual sides are cut **(PHOTO A, on p. 82)**. Unlike the corner matching in earlier projects, the book-matched stock allows all four corners to match, as you can see by examining the grain of the finished box on p. 80. I mark each piece with an arrow pointing toward the top of the box. After they're cut, I number each piece in sequence around the perimeter of the box.

6. Use a sled on the tablesaw to cut the box ends to exact length. Use a stop block to control the length of the cut **(PHOTO B)**.

7. Change the location of the stop block to cut the front and back of the box to length.

Mark and cut the lap-corner joints

WORK SMART

When laying out joinery on two mating parts, use a pencil to mark out the first parts. Once the first parts are cut, mark the mating parts directly off the already-cut parts. When marking the mating parts, using a knife provides greater accuracy.

LAP CORNERS ARE RELATIVELY EASY TO cut and assemble. With a good fit, they will hold together with only a bit of glue. If the fit is a bit loose, the joints can be strengthened by adding interlocking dowels to reinforce the glue. Also, if done well, the finished box can be assembled without the use of clamps, as the friction of a good fit will hold the corners as the glue dries. Most important, cutting lap

LAY OUT THE LAP CORNERS
Use a square and pencil to mark the fingers on the sides and ends of the front and back. Marking and cutting both front and back at the same time will be faster and more accurate and allow for a better fit of the box sides.

MARK OUT THE THICKNESS Use a marking gauge to mark the thickness of the stock on the end of each piece. The marking-gauge line helps whether you cut the joinery by hand or on the tablesaw.

corners is a good stepping-stone to marking and cutting dovetails, as it involves many of the same steps. Lap corners can be cut by hand, machine, or using a combination of the two methods. For more on making these cuts at the tablesaw, see "Lap-Corner Joints at the Tablesaw" on pp. 88–89. To mark out the stock for lap corners, you'll need a marking gauge, a square, and a pencil and marking knife.

CUT TWO AT A TIME Beginning with two resawn pieces of stock, lay one on top of the other and cut two pieces of equal length. From one length you'll cut the front and one side; from the other you'll cut the back and one side.

1. Set the marking gauge slightly wider (about 1/32 in.) than the exact thickness of the stock you're using for the box sides. This extra space allows a bit of overlap in the joints, which can be easily sanded flush after the box is assembled. Pull the marking gauge along both ends of each piece (**PHOTO A**).

2. Measure and mark the locations of the half laps on the front and back of the box (**PHOTO B**). You'll mark only the front and back at this point, then mark the sides off the already cut front and back later. The exact spacing of this joint isn't important as long as all the corners match. On my box, I located the laps by measuring up 1 in. from each edge. By cutting only the front and back at this point, you avoid some confusion, but you may also find it useful to mark an "X" on the portion of the stock to be removed. Use a square to mark cut lines on the ends of the stock, then extend the pencil marks down the face side of each piece until they intersect the lines formed by the marking gauge.

3. Use a dozuki saw or dovetail saw to cut the lines in the front and back. The first cuts can be made on two pieces at a time, speeding up and simplifying the process (**PHOTO C**). Be sure to carefully align

A Lap-Cornered Box

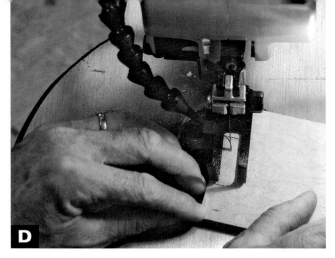

D

CUT THE FINGERS Use a dovetail saw or Japanese dozuki saw to cut down to the marking-gauge line scribed on the ends of the front and back.

the parts in the vise, and take care to follow the marked lines. Pay extra attention to see that the saw is held square to the stock.

4. Remove the waste between cuts. This can be done on the bandsaw, using a coping saw by hand, or with a scrollsaw, as shown in **PHOTO D** at left. Make a sweeping cut into the joint from one direction and then from the other direction. The object is to leave all the cuts just shy of the marking-gauge line, and then clean up the cuts with a chisel.

WORK SMART

When chopping with a chisel, place a piece of scrap plywood on your workbench to avoid making cuts in the benchtop.

E

CHISEL TO THE LINE Use a wide chisel to finish the cut. Fitting it in the marking-gauge line is more a matter of feel than of eyesight, so it is important that the marking-gauge line be well inscribed.

F

MARK THE MATING PARTS Use a knife to mark the fingers on the mating parts. Using a knife is more accurate than a pencil line, but it will be harder to see. Plan to use bright lighting from the side during the cut to increase visibility of the cut line.

G

SAW JUST SHY OF THE LINE Saw down to the marking-gauge line on each piece. To ensure a better fit, cut the sides one at a time. Cut just shy of your mark, leaving about ¹⁄₁₆ in. to be removed with a chisel.

5. Use a chisel to finish the cut. Rest the chisel in the marking-gauge line and give it a few taps with a mallet to begin the cut. Chisel to half depth from one side of the stock, then flip the stock over and cut from the opposite side. To ease assembly, I angle the chisel slightly in toward the stock so that it is slightly undercut (**PHOTO E**). Check the squareness of your cuts using a combination or engineer's square.

6. Mark the box ends directly from the joints cut in the front and back using a marking knife. Clamp the parts tightly together so they don't shift as you apply pressure with the knife. In this application, a marking knife is much more accurate than a pencil.

For the best results, hold the knife flat to the edges of the joint (**PHOTO F**).

7. Saw along the knife marks and then rotate the stock in the vise and cut slightly shy of the marking-gauge lines. In cutting the matching parts, it is best to mark and cut them one at a time. If the cut of the first parts are even the slightest amount out of square, the exact fit will be compromised (**PHOTO G**).

8. Remove the waste as you did on the front and back in step 4. Then use the marking-gauge lines to guide the chisel as you clean up the cuts (**PHOTO H**).

H

CHISEL OUT THE WASTE Chisel in from each side of the stock, trimming exactly on the marking-gauge line. Trying to remove too much waste at a time leads to a poor fit. Chisel to half-depth on one face, then flip the stock and finish the cut from the other side.

Lap corners can be cut accurately and efficiently using a sled on the tablesaw. There is almost always an advantage to using machine tools, and in this case the advantages are obvious. As a production technique, simple setups can result in efficient manufacturing with close tolerances. In cutting this joint, it makes no difference whether you cut the male or female portion first. The secret to a good fit is in careful placement of the stop block.

A CUT TO THE MARKING-GAUGE LINE To cut the lap-corner joints on the tablesaw, use a sled or miter gauge outfitted with a stop block to control the position of the cut. Set the blade to cut along the marking-gauge line and raise the blade to the height you prefer for the lap corners.

1. Use a marking gauge to lay out the thickness of the mating stock on the end of each piece. (This step is no different than when cutting by hand.)

2. Adjust the stop block so that the saw cuts exactly on the marking-gauge line, then raise the blade to the desired height. In this case, the exact height is not critical, but it does determine the width of the male portion of the joint. Make this cut on each corner of the front and back parts (**PHOTO A**).

3. Adjust the stop block and lower the height of the blade so that the cut will intersect the cut you just made at 90 degrees. To avoid trapping waste between the blade and stop block, set the stop block so that you cut on the outside of the male part of the joint (**PHOTO B**).

CUT THE FINGER Set the height of the blade to the thickness of the sides and reset the stop block to locate the fingers of the joint. If your finger is centered on the stock, you'll cut one side of the stock, then simply flip the stock to cut the other.

CUT THE FRONT AND BACK Adjust the stop block to cut the lap joint on the front and back pieces. This cut will require careful measuring for a perfect fit.

MULTIPLE PASSES REMOVE THE WASTE Make a series of cuts to remove the waste between the outside cuts. Cutting to within 1/16 in. of the marking-gauge line will work well if you don't mind a bit of chisel work to finish the fit.

4. With the stock held upright in the sled, make the cut on each side of the joint first **(PHOTO C)**. Then remove the waste material between the cuts, changing the position of the stock on the sled in small increments **(PHOTO D)**. I prefer to cut about 1/16 in. lower than the marking-gauge line, leaving a small amount of stock to be cleaned up with a chisel. Chiseling, rather than sawing, to final depth helps prevent tearout on the back side of the cut.

5. The final fitting of the joint requires a minimal amount of handwork with a chisel. Place the chisel in the marking-gauge line and cut to half depth on one side of the stock. Then flip the stock over to complete the cut **(PHOTO E)**.

CLEAN UP THE CUT As in cutting this joint by hand, set a wide chisel in the marking-gauge line to clean up the cut. Cut in first from the inside face of the stock, then flip the stock over and cut from the other side.

Assemble the sides

FOR THIS BOX, YOU'LL WANT TO ASSEMBLE
the sides of the box before you begin cutting the
lid and base to size. Working in this order, you can
accurately size them for a perfect fit. If you have
done a good job in fitting the lap corners, this box
can be assembled without clamps—the friction of
the fit will hold the parts in position as the glue sets.
A looser fit can be assembled using tape, then reinforced using dowels.

1. Sand the interior surfaces of the box sides to
240 grit. Sanding can be done by hand or machine.
Either way, it's much easier to sand the interior of
the box prior to assembly.

2. Assemble the box parts by applying a small
amount of glue to the surfaces where the male and

female parts of the sides, back, and front join. I
use a squeeze glue dispenser and then spread the
glue evenly on the mating surfaces with my finger
or a stick. Pay attention to the markings on the
box sides to make certain that you assemble all the
parts in the correct order and with the correct sides
facing out.

3. If the joints fit snug, no clamps will be required.
If they are just a bit loose, use clear tape to hold the
parts in position as the glue sets. Even a poorly fitted joint will hold together long enough with glue
and tape for you to install dowels to strengthen the
joints.

4. Check the box for square by measuring corner to
corner and adjust it if necessary before the glue sets.

Make the lid and base

WHETHER YOU CUT THE JOINTS BY HAND
or machine, the steps for making the lid and base
are the same. You'll use a router table with a fence
and a straight-cut router bit. I prefer a rather wide
bit to make the cut, as it cuts more efficiently. As an
alternative, this cut can be made using a dado blade
on the tablesaw. The finished lid and base are each
made in the same manner.

RABBET THE BASE AND LID Fitting the base and
lid can be done on the router table using a wide straight-
cut router bit and a fence to control the position of the
cut. Rout the end grain first so that any tearout on the
sides will be removed in subsequent cuts.

B

FINISH THE RABBET Finish the rabbet on both the top and bottom by routing the sides. As an alternative, this cut can be made using a dado blade on the tablesaw. Cut in small increments to achieve a perfect fit.

1. Cut the top and bottom to length and width at the tablesaw. In this step, you can follow the cutting list or modify the proportions, increasing or decreasing the amount the lid or base extends beyond the sides of the box.

2. With a straight-cut router bit mounted in the router table, raise the bit to cut ⅛ in. high and set the fence so that the router bit is partially buried. The amount of the bit exposed depends on the diameter of the bit you choose. Rout across the end grain first. Any tearout that results where the bit exits the wood will be removed in the next step **(PHOTO A)**. Rather than rout to the finished size based on measurements, I gradually work my way to a perfect fit.

3. Rout the side grain after the end grain. It may help to hold the stock slightly away from the fence for an initial pass. Then finish the cut with the stock held tightly against the fence.

4. Adjust the fence in steps until the base and lid fit within the perimeter of the box sides. An exact fit in length is acceptable. Across the width of the box, allow a small amount of expansion space. In the event that the box is exposed to extreme humidity, this small space will keep expansion of the lid or base from pushing the joints apart **(PHOTO B)**.

When routing multiple edges of a board, always rout the end grain first. Routing the long grain on the sides will remove any tearout created from the end grain cuts.

Shape the lid and base

ROUT THE EDGES Router-bit profiles can be used to rout the edges of the lid and base, or the lid can be shaped using other techniques. At right, a combination of roman ogee and roundover is used, and at left, there is a table-sawn bevel on the lid and a routed chamfer on the base.

MAKING ANY BOX OFFERS MANY CREATIVE options for the box maker. In this case, the simple choice of router bits or methods used in shaping the lid and base can lend unique character to your box. You may want to make more than one of these boxes to gain firsthand knowledge of what works for you and what does not. I follow a few simple guidelines that you are welcome to follow or ignore. If I'm chamfering the edges of a box, I generally use flat surfaces elsewhere to convey a sense of consistency in the design. When using roundover bits or roman ogees, I attempt to use curved edges elsewhere in the piece, to convey the same sense of planned consistency. Following these rules helps create an integrated box design.

1. Use your choice of router bit in the router table to rout the top edges of the lid and the base. I partially bury the bit in the router fence to provide greater control and safety during the cut.

2. Change to a small roundover or chamfering bit to rout the underside of the lid and base.

Finish the box

I PREFER TO ADD THE BASE TO THE BOX after the sides are sanded and all surfaces, including those on the lid, have been finished with Danish oil. Prefinishing allows all surfaces to be well sanded and prevents oil finish from accumulating in corners, where it is difficult to rub out.

As a final creative touch, add hardware of your choice. Look beyond the conventional range of box hardware for some interesting and distinctive results.

Unusual material makes unusual boxes. If you want to make your boxes unique and express your own personality, don't hesitate to experiment with odd or interesting woods. Successful designs grow from trial, error, and experimentation.

ATTACH THE PULL Choose an interesting pull and use screws to attach it to the lid. At left is a solid brass traditional drawer pull used in an unconventional manner. At right is a hand-forged steel pull.

1. Sand the outside surfaces of the box, starting with the stationary belt sander and finishing with the orbital sander with 320 grit paper. If you prefer, the sanding can be done by hand.

2. Sand the lid and base with the orbital sander, then pay special attention to the edges and routed surfaces with a little hand-sanding.

3. Apply two coats of Danish oil. Rub out the finish just before it begins to get sticky, then wait 24 hours before recoating. The object of rubbing out the finish is not to completely dry the surface of the wood, but to wipe away wet spots and distribute the finish in a uniform sheen.

4. Use clear construction adhesive to attach the base to the sides of the box. An alternate approach would be to use wood glue, but this would require masking off the joining surfaces prior to finishing.

5. Install your choice of hardware.

**Building this box from rough woods can add a
rustic charm to a refined design concept.**

THE WALNUT BOX BELOW IS A PERFECT
example of this effect. The contrast between the
coarse texture of the weathered wood against
the refined joints and the smooth, highly polished
texture of the base and lid creates a lasting
impression. To make the rustic walnut box, pass

rough, weathered walnut through the planer with the
textured side turned away from the knives. Thickness
the wood as you would any other lumber, but refrain
from planing the most interesting side of the wood.
Cut the lap joints by hand or at the tablesaw, then
use walnut dowels to secure the joint.

INLAYING THE LID Inlaying various materials—wood or otherwise—into the lid of the box is
another interesting way to personalize the design.
In the box at left above I inlaid landscaping stones
into the lid of a basswood box. But there is no reason to limit yourself to stones—almost any small
object could be inlaid into the lid. When making a
box with this design, the lid must be assembled
from two pieces of wood rather than routed to
fit. While you are at it, it is easy to make the base
using the same assembly technique.

1. Cut two pieces of wood to the dimensions of
the inside of the box and two larger pieces to form
the outside layers of the base and lid.

A

LAY OUT THE STONES Making a lid with inlaid stones
requires careful placement of the rocks and then tracing
their position onto the lid. Once their positions are clearly
marked, draw a meandering line between them.

2. Mark a meandering but pleasing line on the top of the lid panel. Lay your stones in place on the line in an arrangement that suits your tastes, then trace their outlines in pencil **(PHOTO A)**.

3. Use a scrollsaw to cut along the meandering line and then cut away the space within the outlines marked for the stones **(PHOTO B)**.

4. Check the fit of the stones and then gently round the freshly sawn edges of the lid. A round-edged sanding block works great for rounding the edges **(PHOTO C)**.

5. Apply regular woodworking glue to the inner parts of the lid and base. Clamp the outer piece of the base to the inner piece of the base. Then position the two scrollsawn pieces of the top on the inner piece of the top and clamp everything in place **(PHOTO D)**.

6. Before the glue sets, check the fit of the rocks in the lid and make adjustments as necessary **(PHOTO E)**.

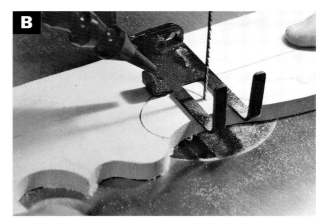

REMOVE STOCK TO FIT THE STONES Use a scrollsaw or coping saw to remove the area to be occupied by the individual stones.

TEST THE FIT Reassemble the top panel temporarily and check the fit of the stones.

GLUE UP THE LID Cover the inner portion of the box lid with glue. This piece should be fitted to the inside dimensions of the box prior to gluing to the top panels.

CLAMP EVERYTHING IN PLACE Use spring clamps to hold the parts of the box lid together while the glue sets.

A Fold-Out Jewelry Box

THIS THREE-TIERED design is based on a Swiss jewelry box given to my daughter by her godmother. The box is both practical and clever, and the original is exquisitely carved. But even without the carving, this design makes a handsome box to house jewelry or any small collection.

Building on skills developed in earlier chapters, this project is challenging but not overwhelming. The basic construction is straightforward: The corners of this box are joined using keyed miter joints like those found on the simple lift-lid box on p. 4. The interior dividers are made using a very simple half-lap technique that can be applied to other projects. Once the box is assembled and finish is applied, the hardware mounts easily to the back of the box.

This box seen here is made of cherry and black mesquite, but the same design can work in almost any pleasing combination of hardwoods. If you build the box or top panel out of basswood, this project becomes a good canvas for the beginning woodcarver.

Three-tiered jewelry box

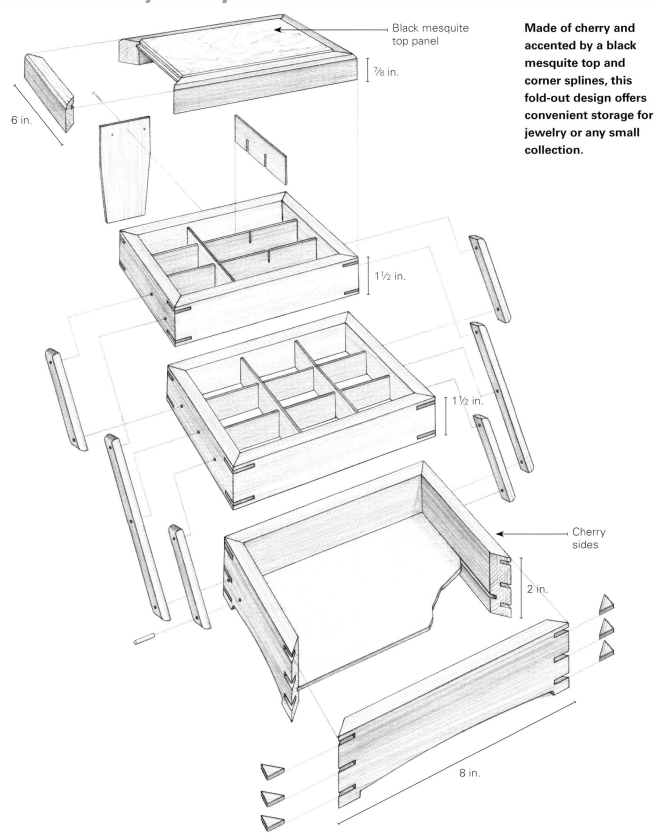

Black mesquite top panel

7/8 in.

6 in.

Made of cherry and accented by a black mesquite top and corner splines, this fold-out design offers convenient storage for jewelry or any small collection.

1 1/2 in.

1 1/2 in.

Cherry sides

2 in.

8 in.

Template for drilling holes

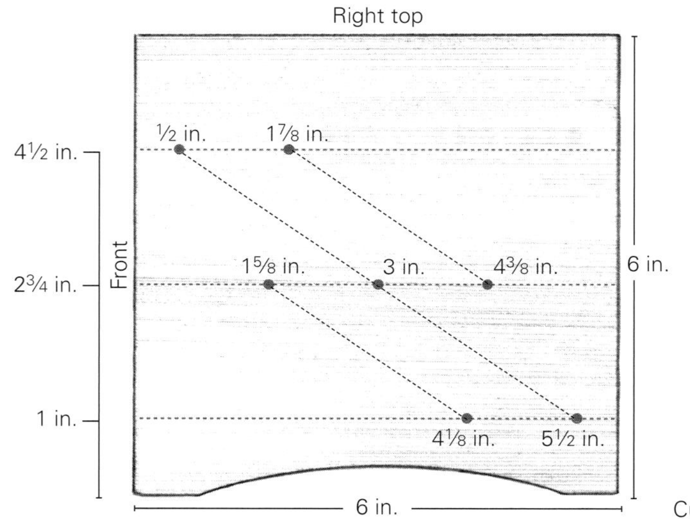
Right top
4½ in.
2¾ in.
1 in.
Front
½ in.
1⅞ in.
1⅝ in.
3 in.
4⅜ in.
4⅛ in.
5½ in.
6 in.
6 in.

All measurements made from front and bottom edges.

Guide for cutting sides

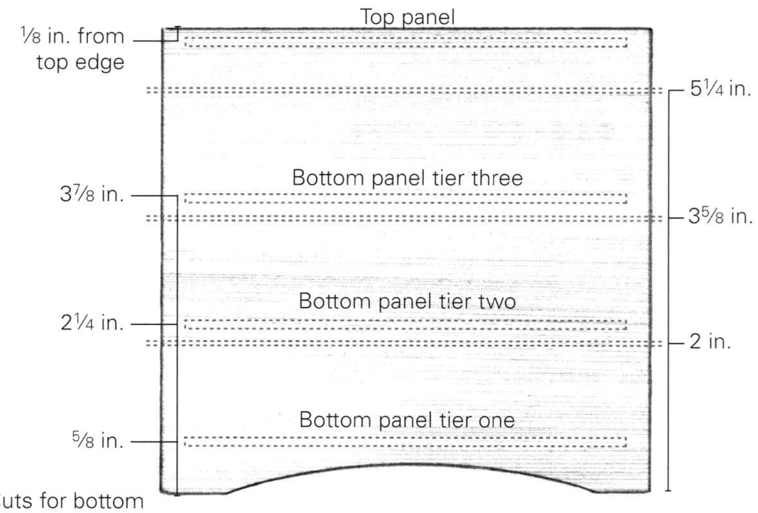
Top panel
⅛ in. from top edge
5¼ in.
Bottom panel tier three
3⅞ in.
3⅝ in.
Bottom panel tier two
2¼ in.
2 in.
Bottom panel tier one
⅝ in.

Cuts for bottom panels made on insides of box parts prior to assembly; measure from base.

Box cut into four sections after assembly; measure from base.

MATERIALS

QUANTITY	PART	ACTUAL SIZE	CONSTRUCTION NOTES
2	Front and back	½ in. x 6¼ in. x 8 in.	Cherry
2	Ends	½ in. x 6¼ in. x 6 in.	Cherry
1	Top panel	7⁄16 in. x 5½ in. x 7½ in.	Black mesquite
3	Bottom panels	⅛ in. x 5½ in. x 7½ in.	Baltic birch plywood
32	Miter keys	⅛ in. x ½ in. x 1 in.	Cherry
4	Support arms (short)	5⁄16 in. x ⅝ in. x 3¾ in.	Cherry
2	Support arms (long)	5⁄16 in. x ⅝ in. x 6⅞ in.	Cherry
1	Back support	5⁄16 in. x 2¾ in. x 5⅛ in.	Cherry
4	Dividers (short)	⅛ in. x 1⅛ in. x 5 in.	Cherry
4	Dividers (long)	⅛ in. x 1 in. x 7 in.	Cherry
17	Screws	#4 brass, ¾ in.	
1 pair	Hinges	¾ wide x 1 in. open	Ives® #C9012B3
4	Linings	5 in. x 7 in.	Ultrasuede or your choice of fabrics

Prepare the stock

THE TALL SIDES OF THIS BOX ARE BEYOND the range of resawing for most tablesaws, and even beyond the range of many small bandsaws. But there is an easy solution. You can use the tablesaw to make partial cuts on both edges of the stock, then finish cutting the stock apart using a handsaw. To avoid resawing altogether, you could also plane stock to a thickness of ½ in. I prefer resawing, however, because the offcuts from resawing come in handy for making the interior dividers.

Only flat stock should be used for this operation—severely warped or crooked stock should be jointed and planed to thickness without resawing.

1. Set the tablesaw fence ⅝ in. from the blade and cut partway into the edge of the stock using a thin-kerf blade. Flip the stock end for end, keeping the same side against the fence, and make another cut along the opposite edge. You may need to take more than one pass on each edge, raising the blade between cuts. Once you're finished cutting, you'll be left with a bit of uncut stock between the two cuts **(PHOTO A)**.

2. Secure the stock in a vise and use a handsaw to finish the cut. You'll need to modify the position of the stock in the vise at various points during the cut. Be sure to save the offcut stock, which you can use for interior dividers later **(PHOTO B)**.

3. Plane the stock to a thickness of ½ in.

4. Square and straighten one edge of the stock on the jointer, then use the tablesaw to rip it to final width.

RESAWING WIDE STOCK To resaw wide stock at the tablesaw, cut to full depth on each edge. Take care to keep the same side registered against the fence, and raise the blade in small increments, if necessary. With a 10-in. blade, a small amount of stock will remain between the two cuts.

FINISH THE CUT WITH A HANDSAW Use either a Western-style ripsaw or a Japanese-style pullsaw to cut through the remaining stock. The tablesaw cuts will keep the handsaw on track throughout the cut.

Miter the sides

THE MITER SLED IS PARTICULARLY USEFUL when cutting boxes with sides as wide as these. The two runners and secure platform of a sled provide accuracy that is difficult for a miter gauge to match. In cutting the sides to length, you'll first cut the stock in half, then cut a paired front and back as well as two paired ends. Clamping stop blocks to the sled ensures that matching parts match in length exactly.

Cutting the box sides from a single board also allows you to lay out the boards so that you'll have continuous grain around the corners of the finished box. Mark the order and location of each side before you make any of the cuts. The reference marks will come in handy when it comes time to assemble the box.

1. Crosscut the stock exactly in the middle so that the ends and sides can be cut with the same settings of the stop block.

2. Use a miter sled outfitted with a stop block to cut the four sides of the box.

3. Clamp the stop block in place on the right side of the fence to guarantee that opposite matching parts turn out the same length. The first cuts on the front and back are made with the exterior face down on the left side of the sled. The last cuts are made with the exterior face up and the mitered end held in place against the stop block on the right side. **(PHOTO )**

4. Change the position of the stop block and cut matching pieces for the two ends.

WORK SMART

Plan your growth as a box maker to move from the simple to the more complex. Before starting any project, carefully consider the types of skills involved. Over time and with effort, you'll be amazed at your progression.

CUT THE SIDES TO LENGTH Use a stop block to control the lengths of the box ends. Reposition the stop block to cut the front and back.

A

CUT FOR THE BOTTOM PANELS AND TOP PANEL TO FIT With the blade set to cut ¼ in. deep, groove the sides to house the bottoms of all three tiers and the top panel. Because you'll need to know the exact locations of these cuts after assembly, mark their locations on the exterior faces of all four sides.

Cut grooves to house the bottom panels

IN ORDER FOR THE BOX TO BE CUT APART into the three tiered sections later, careful planning and measuring is required to position the grooves that house the bottoms. Refer closely to the drawing on p. 97 for the precise measurements. Because these cuts will be invisible on the outside of the box once it's assembled, you'll need to mark the locations of the bottom panels clearly on the outside of the box so you can reference them when you cut apart the three sections.

1. Raise the blade of the tablesaw ¼ in. above the top of the tablesaw. I use a combination blade that has a flat-bottomed cut because it fits the thickness of the ⅛-in. Baltic birch plywood used for the bottoms. Mark out your first cut and then groove all four sides of the box.

2. Continue cutting the other two grooves on the box sides, adjusting your measurements to correspond with the various positions of the bottoms, and cut a similar groove for the top panel **(PHOTO A)**.

3. Rip and crosscut the bottom panels from ⅛-in. Baltic birch plywood.

Make the top panel

FORM THE TONGUE ON THE TOP PANEL using the tablesaw. For this cut, the blade is raised ⅜ in. above the top of the saw and the fence is set ¼ in. from the outside of the blade.

1. Make the first cut with the panel face down on the saw. Cut across the end grain first, then cut the long grain on the sides of the panel **(PHOTO A)**.

2. Lower the blade on the saw to ¼ in. and set the fence so that there is a ⅛-in. space between it and the inside of the blade. Take a practice cut on scrap stock, test the fit in the groove, and adjust the fence as necessary **(PHOTO B)**.

BEGIN MAKING THE TOP PANEL Begin forming the tongue on the top panel by making a cut in the top side of the top panel. The panel in the foreground shows the completed first step.

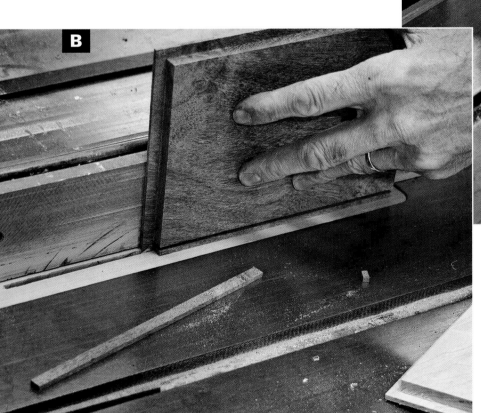

FINISH CUTTING THE TONGUE To complete the tongue on the top panel, cut through to your previous cut with the panel held on edge with the underside against the fence. Set the distance from the blade to the fence so that a ⅛-in. tongue remains. Check the fit of the tongue in the box side and adjust as necessary.

Shape the sides

FEET ARE SHAPED INTO THE FOUR CORNERS of this box, lending it a more distinctive shape and providing a sense of definition from whatever surface the box rests upon. To form the feet, curves are cut into the four sides of the box.

1. Use scissors to cut a template for half of the curve. Keep in mind that the curve must be shallow enough that the cut won't interfere with the groove cut for the bottom.

2. Position the template on one end of the side and mark out the profile. Flip the template over, reposition it on the other end of the side, and mark out the remainder of the curve. If necessary, you can use a pen to create a more visible and distinct line **(PHOTO A)**.

3. Use a scrollsaw to cut the shape in each of the parts. A bandsaw with a fine blade could be used for this step, but a scrollsaw makes such a fine cut that very little sanding is required after cutting **(PHOTO B)**.

4. Clamp the front and back together to sand the surfaces of the scrollsaw cuts, then place the sides together and sand them as well. Sanding matching parts at the same time prevents rounding the bottom edges of the box **(PHOTO C)**.

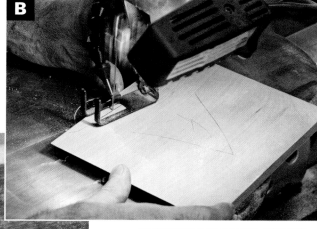

CUT THE SIDES TO SHAPE Use a scrollsaw to make the curved cuts at the base of each side. A bandsaw can make the same cuts, but the rougher edges will require more sanding.

MARK THE SIDES TO FORM THE FEET Use a simple template to mark out the four sides of the box to shape. To create a symmetrical pattern, mark out half the profile, then flip the template over to mark the other end.

SAND THE CUT PROFILES A piece of sandpaper wrapped around a stick with rounded corners makes a perfect sanding tool for this type of cut. Sanding two sides at a time prevents unintended rounding.

Sand the interior

SANDING THE INTERIOR OF THE BOX PRIOR to finishing is much easier than trying to work sandpaper into the corners of an already assembled box. I use an inverted orbital sander to sand the inside surfaces of the box parts, including the sides, top panel, and Baltic birch bottom panels. Although the orbital sander is much faster, hand-sanding will work also. Begin sanding with 180 grit and progress through to 320 grit **(PHOTO A)**.

SAND THE INSIDES BEFORE ASSEMBLY An inverted orbital pad sander works well to sand the inside surfaces of the lid, sides, and bottoms. Sanding by hand will also be effective. Use a sanding block to keep the surface level.

Assemble the box

MITER JOINTS LIKE THE ONES USED IN THIS box can be glued up using little more than tape and rubber bands to hold parts together as the glue dries. In fact, it's difficult to even use clamps on a mitered box, because it's almost impossible to apply a consistent amount of pressure from each clamp.

1. Lay the parts out on the workbench with the outer faces up, then align the corners. If you've cut parts from a single board, be sure that your grain matches from one corner to the next. Apply clear packing tape at each of the three touching corners.

2. Turn the box parts over and spread glue on the mitered surfaces.

3. Place the top panel in the saw kerf at the top of the box, on one side. Then place the Baltic birch bottom panels in place as well.

4. Gradually wrap the sides and ends into place around the top and bottom panels. Then use tape to close and secure the last joint.

5. Use rubber bands or additional wrappings of tape to increase the clamping pressure.

6. Check to see that the box is square by measuring corner to corner across the two diagonals. If the box is square, the measurements will be the same from each direction. If not, make small adjustments using hand pressure.

Cut and install miter keys

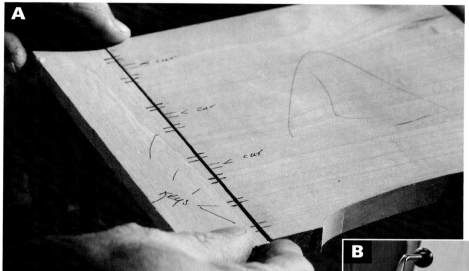

PLAN FOR THE MITER KEYS The box is marked showing the locations of both the miter keys and the cuts for separating the box into three compartments. For setting up the miter-key-slot jig, mark the story stick so that only the locations of the keys are indicated.

INSTALLING MITER KEYS IN A BOX OF THIS size requires a secure platform for carrying the box safely and accurately across the sawblade. With great care, the miter slots could be cut using the simple jig shown on p. 16, but after putting in all the work it takes to make this box, I prefer to take few chances.

As with positioning the cuts for the box bottoms, special care is required to position the key slots. I lay out the key-slot locations using a story stick of wood cut in length to match the height of the box. A stop block clamped in place on the miter key sled makes certain that each key slot will be placed accurately.

1. Use the story stick to plan the locations of your key-slot cuts. Note in **PHOTO A** that I've marked out the spots where the three sections of the box will be cut apart. This information is helpful in placing the keys.

2. Use the key slots marked on your story stick to position the stop block on the miter-key sled.

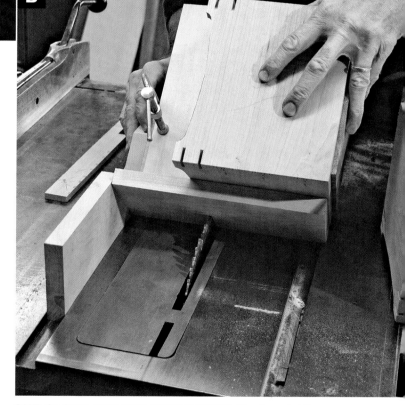

CUT SLOTS FOR THE MITER KEYS The key-slot jig carries the box safely and securely over the blade. Pass the jig through the cut and then return it to the starting position before lifting the box from the jig.

There are numerous slotting jigs used to guide boxes at a 45-degree angle across the blade. This one is simple to make and use. It's also a design I rely on repeatedly in my shop. Because this jig provides solid backing as the blade exits the cut, it provides a cleaner cut than jigs that simply hold the box at a 45-degree angle and are dependent on the fence to control the position of the cut.

1. To begin making the jig, glue two pieces of hardwood into a long "L" shape, as shown in the drawing on the facing page. I use air nails to attach the corners on this jig, angling the nails slightly away from the edge to allow the corner to be chamfered on the tablesaw. If you don't have a pneumatic nailer, glue and clamp the boards in place before driving nails with a hammer.

2. Set the sawblade to 45 degrees and chamfer the corner of the cradle, removing just enough stock so that the cradle will rest on edge for the next steps. The flattened corner will also provide greater stability when you use the jig (**PHOTO A**).

3. Plane a piece of hardwood stock to slide in the miter slot of your saw. I work my way down to a perfect fit in small increments and go by feel rather than by measurements.

CUT THE CORNER After the box cradle is assembled, flatten the corner to ride on the surface of the tablesaw top. Tilt the blade to 45 degrees for this cut.

MARK THE RUNNER With the runner set into the miter slot on your tablesaw, mark the shape of the cradle onto the side of the runner.

CUT TO THE LINES Angle the blade to 45 degrees, then cut the shape of the cradle using a miter gauge on your tablesaw.

ATTACH THE CRADLE TO THE RUNNER Position the runner in the miter slot, then clamp the cradle in place. Predrill for screws and then assemble the jig.

4. Put the finished runner in the miter slot and hold it in position while tracing the inside shape of the carriage (**PHOTO B**).

5. Raise the blade on the tablesaw and set the angle to 45 degrees, then cut the profile of the carriage into the guide strip. Removing this material will provide clearance for attaching stop blocks and allow for easy alignment during assembly. Make the cut in two steps—one from each side—but leave the sawcut just shy of the final height. This will leave the triangle-shaped block affixed to the guide piece rather than loose, which can be an invitation for kickback from the saw (**PHOTO C**).

6. After the waste is broken away, hand-chisel any remaining wood at the center of the cut.

7. Use clamps to hold the "V" carriage in place and attach it to the guide strip using 1⅝-in. drywall screws (**PHOTO D**).

Miter key sled for large boxes

This durable sled holds large boxes securely in position for cutting spline slots on the corners of boxes.

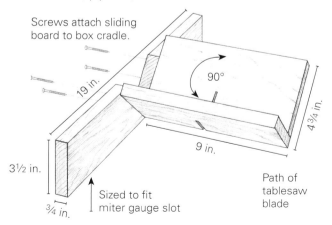

Use stop block and C-clamps to position box on sled
Hardwood, plywood, or MDF.

Screws attach sliding board to box cradle.

90°

19 in.

4¾ in.

9 in.

3½ in.

¾ in.

Sized to fit miter gauge slot

Path of tablesaw blade

¾-in.-thick board rides in miter gauge slot on tablesaw.

INSTALL THE MITER KEYS Dip the edges of each miter key in glue before inserting it in its key slot. Pushing the key in place helps distribute the glue.

3. Use the miter key sled to cut the miter-key slots. Rotate the box to cut at each corner, and then change the location of the stop block to make the next set of cuts (**PHOTO B on p. 105**).

4. Refer to the first project in this book, "A Simple Lift-Lid Box," for instructions on making miter keys. You can use wood that matches the sides of the box, or use a contrasting wood. Glue and set the miter keys in place. After the glue sets, sand the keys flush with the sides of the box (**PHOTO C**).

Cut the lid and levels apart

CUTTING THE LID AND THREE TIERS OF THE box into separate parts requires careful measuring and cutting.

1. Set the height of the blade just a hair lower than the thickness of the box sides so that the box will stay together after each cut. Judge the correct thickness by making the first cut slightly low and then trying to pierce through the remaining wood with a box-cutting knife. If it goes through too easily, I lower the blade slightly. If it's too difficult to cut, I raise the blade just a little.

2. Use the markings on the box sides to guide setting up the distance between the fence and the blade for each set of cuts (**PHOTO A**).

CUT THE BOX APART Set the height of the blade so that it leaves just a bit of stock uncut on each side. Check the depth of the cut by poking through with a razor or X-Acto® knife. It should take only a little pressure to cut through the remaining wood.

Fit the support arms

THE ARMS THAT CONNECT THE LEVELS OF the box and control their movement must be positioned just right for the box to open and close properly. I make a single drilling template to help position matching holes on both ends of the box. Carefully position the template on one end and then the other. Make sure you keep the same edge up and the same edge toward the front while marking each end.

1. Make the template from ⅛-in. Baltic birch plywood or Masonite®. Cut the template to the exact size of the box after it has been cut into three tiers and the lid has been cut loose. Mark the front edge and top edge of the template on each side, then mark the location of each box tier and the lid on the template. Drill ¹⁄₁₆-in. holes through the plywood to make a reversible drilling guide. Refer to the drawing

MAKE A DRILLING TEMPLATE To locate the holes used to attach the support arms to the ends of the box, make a template from plywood cut to the exact size of the box end. Use a drill press and fence to drill the holes.

DRILL THE BOX ENDS Clamp the template in place on the box end, then use a self-centering bit (called a vix bit) to drill the holes. This operation can be done with a standard drill bit, but take care to see that you don't drill too deep. Drill holes ¼ in. deep.

FLIP THE TEMPLATE FOR A MIRROR IMAGE Flip the template over and align it with the other end of the box to drill a mirror-image pattern of holes on the opposite end. Be certain that the front edge of the template aligns with the front edge of the box.

on p. 98 for the exact positions of the holes. I used a drill press equipped with a fence to gain the greatest accuracy in drilling holes (**PHOTO A**).

2. Position the template on the right side of the box and use a self-centering drill bit to drill pilot holes directly through the template. To avoid shifting either the template or the box, clamp the whole assembly to your workbench. Make certain that the front edge and top edge of the template align with the front edge and top edge of the box (**PHOTO B**).

3. After drilling one end of the box, flip the box over and repeat the same steps on the other end of the box. Again, be careful that the front edge and top edge of the template align with the front edge and top edge of the box (**PHOTO C**).

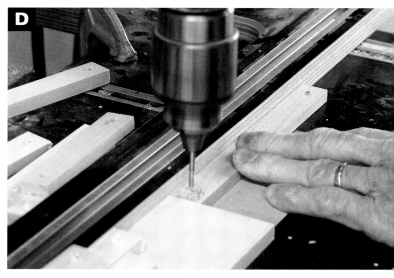

DRILL THE SUPPORT ARMS Use the drill press to drill mounting holes in the support arms. The fence in combination with stop blocks makes it easy to position the holes.

COUNTERSINK THE HOLES
Use a countersink bit to finish drilling the holes in the support arms. Set the depth so that the head of the screw sits flush to the face of the support arms.

F

ROUT THE SUPPORT ARMS Use a ³⁄₁₆-in.-radius roundover bit in the router table to shape the ends of the support arms. Routing the ends held together in a group makes this process easier and more accurate. Beginners should use tape to hold the parts together for this operation.

4. Drill ⅛-in. holes through the support arms using a drill press. Use a fence and stop block to control the position of the holes. You'll need to reposition the stop block to drill holes in the center of the middle support **(PHOTO D , on p. 109)**.

5. Countersink the holes in the supports using a countersink bit in the drill press. Adjust the drill press depth so the countersink allows for a #4 screw to fit flush with the surface. Check the fit of a screw in the hole to fine-tune the depth of the countersink **(PHOTO E)**.

6. Shape the ends of the support arms using a ³⁄₁₆-in. roundover bit in the router table. I hold several pieces together at a time to reduce tearout during the routing operation **(PHOTO F)**.

Make the rear support

THE REAR SUPPORT ATTACHES TO THE BACK of the box and is sized to keep the box level as the various layers separate and spread when the box is opened. It is attached with three countersunk brass wood screws.

1. Plane the stock to thickness and cut it to size and length, then cut angled sides on the support using a sled with an angled fence. The sides of the rear support can be angled using a conventional miter gauge, but I prefer a sled with a nail-in-place temporary fence because it pulls the support back safely from the blade when the cut is completed **(PHOTO A)**. This useful sled is made in the same manner as my other sleds, except it has no fence. For this operation, I simply screw on a temporary fence at the 5-degree angle required and tack the stop block in place. To try this technique with an existing sled, use screws to attach an angled strip in front of the regular fence, then tack a stop block in place to position the workpiece.

A

ADD AN ANGLED JIG TO A CROSS-
CUT SLED Taper the rear support using a
crosscut sled with a temporary angled fence
tacked or screwed in place. This task could
also be done using a miter gauge, but the
sled is much safer. A stop block nailed to the
sled positions the workpiece.

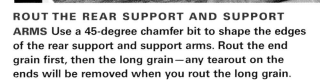

2. Shape the rear support on the router table
using a chamfering bit set to cut about ⅛ in. deep
(PHOTO B). While you are set up with this bit in
the router table, go ahead and chamfer the outside
edges of the support arms. As shown in the photos,
the ends of the support arms were routed with a
³⁄₁₆-in. roundover bit in the router table.

B

**ROUT THE REAR SUPPORT AND SUPPORT
ARMS** Use a 45-degree chamfer bit to shape the edges
of the rear support and support arms. Rout the end
grain first, then the long grain—any tearout on the
ends will be removed when you rout the long grain.

Make the dividers

A

THE DIVIDERS USED INSIDE THIS BOX FIT
together using interlocking half-lap joints. You
essentially cut a slot onto each mating divider, then
slide the two parts together. For the interlocking
half-lap joints to fit together smoothly, the length of
the stock needs to be accurate. I use a crosscut sled
on the tablesaw to cut dividers to length and to cut
the interlocking joints.

MAKE THE INTERIOR DIVIDERS Half-depth cuts
in the dividers interlock to form compartments inside
the box. Clamp stop blocks in place to control the
position of each divider. Make one cut with the divider
against the stop block on the left, then make another
with the stock against the block on the right.

ROUT THE DIVIDERS The top edges of the dividers are rounded using a ¹⁄₁₆-in.-radius roundover bit at the router table. Rout one top edge with the stock held upright against the fence and pilot bearing. Then flip the stock to rout the other side of the top edge.

B

1. After thicknessing the stock at the planer, cut the dividers to length using a crosscut sled at the tablesaw.

2. Cut the half laps in the parts by holding them upright against the sled fence and moving them between the stop blocks. Using two stop blocks on the sled allows you to widen the cut slightly to fit the width of the stock. I take one pass with the stock hard to the right stop block, then shift it over to the left, effectively and accurately widening the cut.

Change the locations of the stop blocks to cut the half laps in the mating parts (**PHOTO A**, on p. 111).

3. Use a ¹⁄₁₆-in. roundover bit in the router table to rout the top edges of the divider parts. Remember that the parts going one way get routed with the cut side down. The matching parts get routed with the cut side up. Note how the crosspieces are cut narrower to provide a more interesting intersection of parts (**PHOTO B**).

Sand, finish, and assemble

BEFORE ASSEMBLING THIS BOX, YOU'LL want to give all the parts a good sanding. I sand the cut lines between the three tiers of the box using sheets of sandpaper held face up on a flat surface, progressing from 150 to 320 (**PHOTO A**). The box sides can be sanded with an orbital sander, but it helps to keep the sections of the box held tightly together on a cushioned surface during sanding. The support arms, back support, and dividers should

WORK SMART

Hand-sanding small parts is more effective and accurate than machine sanding. Wrap a stick with sandpaper to sand details on small stock. For shaped stock, used a shaped stick that mimics the profile you're trying to sand.

be sanded by hand. I use a stick wound with a sandpaper scrap to sand edges and routed surfaces (**PHOTO B**).

Danish oil is my preferred finish for this box, and it is significantly easier to apply the finish before final assembly. Once the finish has dried, use brass screws to attach the support arms to the sides of the box (**PHOTO C**). To attach the rear support to the top level of the box, position it at the center of the back of the box and use an awl to locate the position of the pilot holes. Then predrill and install brass screws to hold it in place (**PHOTO D**).

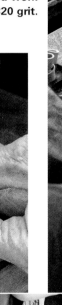

SMOOTH THE CUT LINES Hand-sand the edges of the box sections using sheets of sandpaper on a flat surface. The top of your tablesaw works well. Start with 150 grit and work your way to 240 and 320 grit.

SAND THE ENDS AND EDGES Use a piece of sandpaper wrapped around a thin stick of wood to sand the chamfered edges of the support arms and rear support.

ATTACH THE SUPPORT ARMS Before installing the support arms to the side of the box, align the three sections of the box and clamp them together. Be careful not to overtighten the brass screws used to attach the arms. A bit of beeswax applied to the screws helps them go in smoothly.

MARK FOR THE BACK SUPPORT Use an awl to mark the locations of the screws for the back support. Standing the box upright aligns the back support with the bottom edge of the box. Predrill the screw holes before attaching the back support.

Hinge the lid

THE BRASS HINGES USED ON THIS BOX
came from my local hardware store. They're inexpensive and easy to install, but require a small warning. Small brass screws like the ones used in these hinges are notorious for breaking off in hardwoods as they're installed. Be sure you predrill the holes to the right size and lubricate the screw threads with beeswax prior to driving them home.

1. Use a clamp to hold the lid and base in position. It is important to allow a small space between the lid and the base so that the hinges don't bind at the rear of the box. A piece of card stock placed between the lid and base provides the correct clearance. Mark the location for the pilot holes using an awl (**PHOTO A**).

PREDRILL SCREW HOLES Instead of using a drill bit, chuck a nail in your drill and use it to predrill the holes for the screws. The tapered point of a nail better conforms to the shape of the screw. Mark the depth with tape to keep from drilling too deep.

LAY OUT THE HINGE LOCATIONS Hold the hinge securely in place, then mark the center points of the holes with an awl. It is sometimes easier to mark and install one screw at a time.

WORK SMART

Lubricate brass screws with beeswax before driving them into hardwoods. Accurately predrilling holes and using beeswax will keep brass screws from breaking off in the wood.

2. Drill pilot holes in the locations marked. In place of a drill bit, I use a nail chucked up in the drill with the head removed. I also wrap a piece of masking tape around the nail so that I'll know how deep to drill **(PHOTO B)**.

3. Wax the screws before insertion, and use a hand screwdriver to drive them home. When driven in with a drill/driver, brass screws have a tendency to shear off easily in hardwoods **(PHOTO C)**.

INSTALL THE BRASS SCREWS
To avoid breaking brass screws as you drive them into hardwoods, coat the threads with a bit of beeswax to ease their entry. Careful sizing of the pilot holes also helps.

WORK SMART

Use a nail in place of a drill bit to bore pilot holes for small screws. The pointed shape of the nail leaves a hole that better conforms to the shape of the screw, making it easier for the screw to begin threading in the hole.

Cut and install a lining

FLOCKED MATERIAL, ULTRASUEDE, HAND-MADE paper, and a variety of other materials can be used as box linings. All of these materials are easily cut to size using a common quilter's tool available from sewing supply dealers. You could use a razor knife instead, but the quilter's tool won't pull at the fabric like a razor knife. In a pinch, scissors can work also.

1. Cut a template from thin plywood or Masonite to the exact dimensions of the interior of the box.

2. Hold the template tightly in place over the lining material while you roll the cutter along the edges **(PHOTO A)**.

CUT THE LININGS TO SIZE Use a rotary cutter and wooden template to cut linings for the box interiors. Hold the template firmly in place, then roll the cutter along the edge. The template is sized to the exact dimensions of the interior of the box. With care, a razor knife will make the same cut.

Try mixing contrasting hardwoods to add color and complexity to
the top of your box. Carving is also an option when stylizing this project.

CREATE A MULTICOLORED LID

1. Start with two contrasting hardwoods milled to
⅝ in. thick, ¼ in. wider than the final dimensions
of the top panel, and long enough to pass safely
through the planer.

2. Use double-stick tape to hold the two pieces
of contrasting wood in a stack so that the two
panels don't shift around as you make sweeping cuts
through the layers. Tight curves should be avoided
(PHOTO A, BELOW LEFT).

3. Peel the tape from between the layers, and then
mix and match the parts to achieve a contrasting
pattern.

4. Fill the saw kerfs with contrasting veneers,
layered in thickness to the width of the saw kerf.
This will fill voids when the pattern is glued together.
(PHOTO B).

5. Plane the patterned wood to its final thickness
and make your top panel in the same manner as
described in making the cherry and mesquite box.

MAKE A MIXED HARDWOOD TOP Use the
bandsaw to cut through two layers of different species of hardwoods. Cutting a simple pattern with
gentle curves guarantees success.

GLUE UP THE TOP Spread glue between the cuts
and add thin veneers to fill the saw kerf left by the
bandsaw. Mix and match the hardwoods and veneers
to create an interesting contrast of woods.

DESIGN YOUR CARVING Plan your carving using a template to arrange a random floral pattern. Then sketch in vines and leaves, starting on the front of the box and leading over the edge and onto the top.

ADD HAND-CARVED DETAILS

When made of basswood, this box presents an excellent opportunity to practice your carving skills. I chose a simple pattern of petunias, vines, and leaves for this box.

1. Cut a simple template to help mark out your design. Sketching petunias may be difficult for some, so beginners may want to try a heart or other shape that is easily cut with a pair of scissors. The pattern I use evolved over time by looking at books and continually simplifying what I saw to very basic shapes. Remember that simple is your best starting point when learning a new skill.

2. Use the template to begin marking out the pattern. A simple, random arrangement works best. Use a pen to trace the template at various locations, then draw in simple vines to connect them. Add leaves wherever they seem appropriate (**PHOTO C**).

3. Use a small straight chisel to cut lines isolating the foreground objects from the background. Then use a shallow gouge to begin removing the background. Cut in to the lines cut with the straight chisel and then gradually remove stock to a planned border area (**PHOTO D**).

4. Use a small gouge and V-parting tool to add additional details. Keep the box held together with rubber bands throughout the carving process. After the carving is complete, lightly sand the background with fine sandpaper (**PHOTO E**).

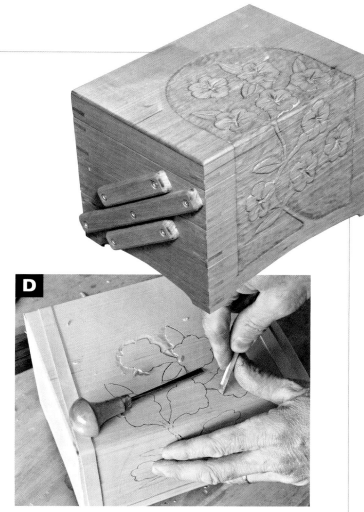

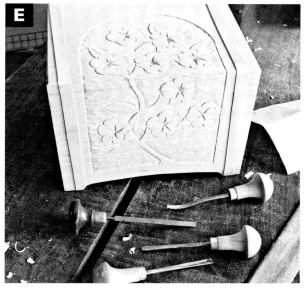

CARVE THE PATTERN A straight chisel cuts the outline of the design and a shallow gouge removes the background. Only shallow cuts are necessary.

FINISHING TOUCHES Use a deeper gouge and a V-gouge to add details to the leaves and flowers.

A Jewelry Box
with a Sliding Tray

LTHOUGH ANY BOX can be adapted to a number of uses, the safe storage of jewelry is one of the most common uses for a finely crafted wooden box. This design, made of walnut and pecan, is rather simple as jewelry boxes go, but building the sliding tray and interior dividers of this box presents a great opportunity to explore options for box interiors. This design is built using many of the same techniques used in earlier chapters, but offers a few twists to expand your range of design and construction techniques.

Using angled keys to reinforce the miter joints creates a visual tension and adds even greater beauty to the corners of the box. The simple mitered tray is made using the same techniques used in making the first box in this book. Using solid brass hinges with a built-in stop completes the project. To install the hinges, you'll use an easy and accurate technique on the router table, simplifying an otherwise demanding task.

A sliding tray refines this design

This box was designed to be a jewelry box, but the same or a slightly altered design could be used to house any small collection.

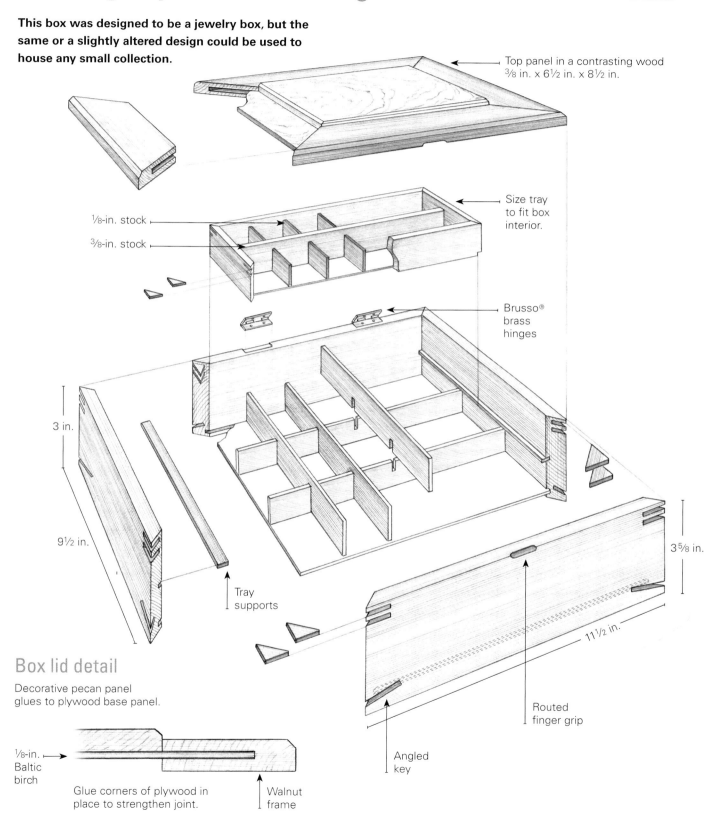

Top panel in a contrasting wood
3/8 in. x 6 1/2 in. x 8 1/2 in.

Size tray to fit box interior.

1/8-in. stock

3/8-in. stock

Brusso® brass hinges

3 in.

9 1/2 in.

Tray supports

3 5/8 in.

11 1/2 in.

Routed finger grip

Angled key

Box lid detail

Decorative pecan panel glues to plywood base panel.

1/8-in. Baltic birch

Glue corners of plywood in place to strengthen joint.

Walnut frame

MATERIALS

QUANTITY	PART	ACTUAL SIZE	CONSTRUCTION NOTES
2	Front and back	$^9/_{16}$ in. x 3 in. x 11$^1/_2$ in.	Walnut
2	Sides	$^9/_{16}$ in. x 3 in. x 9$^1/_2$ in.	Walnut
12	Miter keys	$^1/_8$ in. x $^3/_4$ in.	Walnut, lengths may vary
2	Lid front and back	$^5/_8$ in. x 1$^1/_2$ in. x 11$^1/_2$ in.	Walnut
2	Lid sides	$^5/_8$ in. x 1$^1/_2$ in. x 9$^1/_2$ in.	Walnut
1	Lid core panel	$^1/_8$ in. x 8$^1/_2$ in. x 10$^1/_2$ in.	$^1/_8$ in.-thick Baltic birch plywood
1	Lid panel	$^3/_8$ in. x 6$^1/_2$ in. x 8$^1/_2$ in.	Pecan
1	Bottom	$^1/_4$ in. x 8$^7/_8$ in. x 10$^7/_8$ in.	$^1/_8$ in.-thick Baltic birch plywood
2	Divider parts A	$^1/_8$ in. x 1 in. x 10$^3/_8$ in.	Walnut
3	Divider parts B	$^1/_8$ in. x 1$^1/_8$ in. x 8$^3/_8$ in.	Walnut
2	Tray supports	$^1/_8$ in. x $^3/_8$ in. x 8$^3/_8$ in.	Walnut
2	Tray front and back	$^5/_{16}$ in. x 1$^1/_2$ in. x 10$^5/_{16}$ in.	Walnut
2	Tray sides	$^5/_{16}$ in. x 1$^1/_2$ in. x 4$^1/_2$ in.	Walnut
1	Tray bottom	$^1/_8$ in. x 4$^1/_8$ in. x 9$^{15}/_{16}$ in.	Baltic birch
1	Tray divider	$^3/_8$ in. x 1 in. x 9$^3/_4$ in.	Walnut
3	Tray dividers	$^1/_8$ in. x $^3/_4$ in. x 3$^3/_4$ in.	Walnut
8	Miter keys	$^1/_8$ in. x $^1/_2$ in. x $^7/_8$ in	Pecan
1	Mirror	6$^7/_{16}$ in. x 8$^7/_{16}$ in.	Single- or double-strength glass
1 pair	Hinges	1$^1/_4$ in. long x $^5/_8$ in. wide (closed)	Brusso hinges, available from www.woodcraft.com or www.rockler.com

Prepare the stock

UNLIKE MANY OF THE BOXES IN THIS BOOK, resawing stock for this project is not an option unless you have particularly thick stock. Start by planing the material for the sides to $^9/_{16}$ in. thick and the materials for the lid to $^5/_8$ in. Once it's planed to thickness, edge joint and rip the material to finished width.

Cut miters for the lid and base

CUTTING THE LID AND BASE IS QUITE EASY using two different methods on the tablesaw. I cut the sides using the miter sled and a stop block to control the length of cut. There are many ways to make a frame-and-panel lid, but the method used here is one of the easiest. In this technique, a piece of ⅛-in. Baltic birch plywood provides a foundation for attaching a decorative panel of figured wood. The plywood panel also provides a secure means of joining the corners, taking the place of biscuits or more complicated joinery techniques. To cut the frame parts for the lid, a standard tablesaw miter gauge works fine.

1. Use the miter sled (for more on the sled, see "Two Versatile Miter Sleds" on pp. 56–57) outfitted with a stop block to cut the front and back parts to length. Adjust the location of the stop block to cut the box sides **(PHOTO A)**.

2. Use a tablesaw miter gauge to cut the mitered frame of the lid. As when you're using the miter sled, stop blocks make certain the front and back and the two sides are exactly the same length **(PHOTO B)**.

A

MITER THE BOX SIDES (LEFT) The miters on the sides of the box are cut using a tablesaw sled to carry the stock through the cut. A stop block clamped in place makes certain that multiple cuts come out to the same length.

MITER THE LID FRAME (BELOW) Use a miter gauge to cut a miter at one end of each piece. Then clamp a stop block in place to cut two matching parts to the same length. Change the location of the stop block to cut the opposite pair.

WORK SMART

Carefully check blade angle when changing from a 45-degree cut to a 90-degree cut or vice versa. Use a combination square or machinist's square to double check the angle of the blade. Even a small degree of inaccuracy can cause trouble for a box maker.

B

Fit panels in
the bottom and lid

GROOVES CUT INTO BOTH THE INSIDE OF
the box and the inside edges of the lid are used to
house the panels for both the bottom of the box and
the lid frame. While you're cutting these grooves,
go ahead and prepare for the fitting of tray supports
after assembly. I do these operations on the tablesaw, adjusting the blade height and fence position
for each cut.

1. Raise the blade height to 1 in. to groove the
inside edges of the lid frame. I set the distance from
the fence to the inside edge of the cut at ¼ in., then
use a push block to control the stock safely through
the cut (**PHOTO A**).

2. To cut the box sides for the bottom panel to fit,
lower the blade height to ¼ in. and set the fence so
that the outside edge of the cut is ¼ in. from the fence.
Pass each piece of the base across the blade with the
inside bottom edge against the fence. Use a push
block to keep your hands safe throughout the cut.

3. The tray on the interior of this box rests on supports set into the ends of the box, which allow it to
slide from the front to the back of the box easily.
The ends of the box are grooved to accept the tray
supports. Keep the blade set at the same height as
for the previous operation, but change the position
of the fence so that the measurement from the fence
to the outside edge of the cut is 1½ in. Make this
cut with the bottom edge of the stock against the
fence (**PHOTO B**).

A

**GROOVE THE
FRAME TO
ACCEPT THE
PANEL** Use a
⅛-in.-kerf sawblade
in the tablesaw and
set the fence so that
there is a ¼-in. space
between it and the
blade. Then groove
the inside edge of
each piece of the lid
frame to a depth of
1 in. The plywood
panel will fit in these
grooves, locking the
mitered corners and
providing a base for a
decorative hardwood
panel.

B

CUT GROOVES TO HOUSE THE TRAY SUPPORTS Adjust the tablesaw so that the distance from the fence to the outside edge of the blade is 1½ in., then groove the ends of the box for tray supports to fit. Cut only the ends of the box, not the front and back.

Cut the top and bottom panels to fit

I USE BALTIC BIRCH PLYWOOD FOR THE TOP and bottom panels in this box. Because plywood is dimensionally stable, resisting wood's natural inclination to change dimensions in response to changes in humidity, it makes a useful structural element for boxes. I use ¼-in. plywood to form the base of this box, but choose lighter-weight ⅛-in. plywood for the lid. Although the plywood for the lid will fit into the ⅛-in. groove cut into the lid frame earlier, the edges of the ¼-in. thick bottom need to be rabbeted to fit the grooves on the box sides.

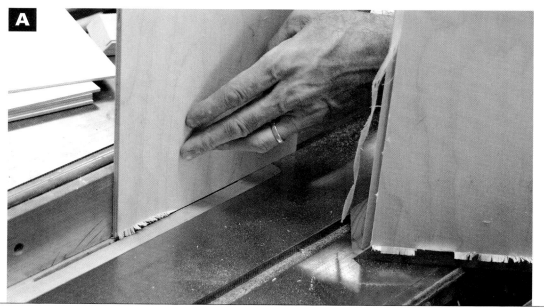

A

FIT THE BOTTOM PANEL Hold the Baltic birch bottom panel on edge to make this cut. Adjust the saw so that there is a ⅛-in. space between the fence and the blade, then hold the ⅛-in. Baltic birch bottom on edge as you make the cut. To reduce tearout, cut the ends of the panel first.

1. Cut the base and lid panels to size. Please note on the materials list on p. 120 that these parts are different sizes. Because your cuts may differ slightly from those listed in the materials list, take your measurements directly from the cut parts.

2. Use the tablesaw to rabbet the edges of the ¼-in. plywood to fit the saw kerfs in the box sides. I set the blade height just over ¼ in. and set the fence so that there is ⅛ in. between the blade and the fence. Hold the stock tightly against the fence and pass the stock over the blade. If you get a rather ragged edge on the cut stock, don't worry—you'll sand the fuzz away prior to assembly **(PHOTO A on p. 123)**.

Carpet samples make great sanding pads and are inexpensive. Check your local carpet dealer. They usually sell carpet samples for a dollar or two, and sometimes they give them away free. Throw them away when they get soiled.

Assemble the sides and lid

IT IS MUCH EASIER TO SAND THE INSIDE OF the box prior to assembly. I lay all the pieces flat on a scrap of carpet and use a half-sheet orbital sander to sand the interior faces, but hand-sanding would work as well. During glue-up, use clear package tape to pull the mitered corners together.

1. Lay out the box sides with their outside faces down and sand them staring with 180 grit and progressing to 240 grit. It's easiest to go ahead and sand the Baltic birch panels at the same time. To sand the inside edges of the lid frame, hold them together and on edge while moving the sander over them **(PHOTO A)**.

SAND THE INTERIOR PRIOR TO ASSEMBLY Use an orbital sander to sand the inside surfaces of all the box parts before assembling the box. Though it's a bit slower, hand-sanding will work also.

GLUE UP THE MITERS With the corners aligned and taped together on the exterior faces of the box, spread glue onto the mitered ends of the box sides. Using a squeeze bottle prevents a mess.

ASSEMBLE THE BOX Once the glue is applied, roll the box sides around the bottom panel. Add tape to pull the last corner tight, then add additional layers of tape to tighten the pressure on all four joints.

2. With the exterior faces of the box facing up, apply clear tape to the corners. Then flip the assembly over and apply glue to the mitered corners and the groove where the bottom fits **(PHOTO B)**.

3. Roll the assembled parts up around the bottom panel, then use clear tape to secure the last corner. Pull the tape tight and apply additional layers as needed at each corner. Additional layers of tape provide additional pressure to the joints **(PHOTO C)**.

4. Use the same technique to glue up the parts for the top frame. Glue applied to each mitered surface and also within the groove creates strong joints **(PHOTO D)**.

GLUE UP THE LID FRAME Spread glue on the miters of the lid frame and in the grooves. Assemble the lid parts around the Baltic birch panel and tape the joints tightly before the glue sets.

Make the top panel

A

MAKE A TOP PANEL
Prepare stock for a decorative top panel using the tablesaw to resaw thicker stock. Raise the blade in increments to its full height, leaving a small amount in the middle to be cut by hand.

B

FINISH THE CUT Use a handsaw to finish the cut. Clamp one end in the vise as you start the cut, then flip the stock over to finish the cut. The sawn groove on both sides will guide the handsaw through the cut.

THIS BOX USES A DECORATIVE FIGURED
pecan panel to contrast with the walnut in the sides and lid frame. This decorative panel is simply glued in place atop the plywood panel after assembly of the lid frame. Because the wood is wider than the capacity of my bandsaw, I used a combination of tablesaw and handsaw to complete the cut. By resawing the thicker pecan stock, I was able to make two top panels from a single piece of hardwood.

1. Raise the blade on the tablesaw to its maximum height and saw in from each edge of the top panel. It helps to leave the stock slightly oversize in width and a great deal oversize in length. Extra length helps guide the wood safely through the cut. Warped stock should be avoided, and a good grip well above the height of the blade is required. You may find it helpful to raise the sawblade in increments rather than trying to make a deep cut all at once (**PHOTO A**).

2. Mount the wood in the vise and use a handsaw (I used a Japanese-style saw) to remove the small amount of material left in the middle of the board. You'll be surprised how quickly the saw passes through the wood, and the sawn surfaces help guide the saw through the cut (**PHOTO B**).

3. Allow the panel to adjust to shop moisture for a few days before planing it to final thickness. After planing, cut the panel to a dimension 1/16 in. narrower in width than the space between the parts of the assembled lid frame.

Cut the slots and install the keys

I USE A MITER-KEY JIG (FOR MORE ON THE jig, see "Making a Miter Key Sled" on pp. 106–107) on the tablesaw to cut the miter-key slots. Because the angled slot cuts reduce the area of support as the blade exits the cut, I make the straight cuts first and save the angled cuts for last. Don't worry, however, about damaging your well-crafted miter-key-slot sled. In the future, you can place a piece of scrapwood over the cut when you use the sled.

1. Clamp a stop block in place on the keyed miter jig to help position the box over the path of the tablesaw cut. To finish cutting all the slots, you'll need to reposition the stop block. Tilt the angle of the blade to make the final cuts **(PHOTO A)**.

2. Rip the key stock to a ⅛ in. thick and then check the fit of the miter-key stock in an actual miter-key slot. Trial and error leads to a near-perfect fit **(PHOTO B , on p. 128)**.

CUT THE KEY SLOTS Use a miter-key jig on the tablesaw to cut the miter-key slots. Tilting the blade at an angle (here, the blade is tilted to about 8 degrees) adds an interesting effect to an already decorative joint.

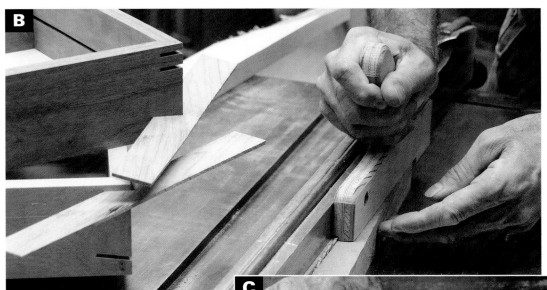

B

CUT MITER-KEY STOCK Use the tablesaw to cut ⅛-in.-thick stock to make the miter keys. Check the actual fit of the stock in the key slots to fine-tune your cut.

C

D

CUT THE KEYS TO LENGTH AND SHAPE Using a low miter sled to cut triangular miter keys means less work trimming them to size once they're installed. To form the triangles, flip the stock over after making your first cut on each key.

3. Use a miter sled on the tablesaw to cut the miter keys to length. Cutting them in a triangular shape reduces the amount of sanding required, and prevents the need to handsaw along the side of the newly assembled box **(PHOTO C)**.

4. Install the keys and sand all the keys flush with the surfaces of the box **(PHOTO D)**.

SAND THE BOX SIDES After the miter keys are installed, use a belt sander to sand the miter keys flush with the box sides. Begin sanding at 150 grit and then move to the orbital sander for a smoother finish. Though slower, hand-sanding will work also.

Rout a finger grip

ROUTING FINGER GRIPS IN THE TOP AND base of this box is quick work. But if you're not paying attention, it's also easy to leave unnecessary tearout on the front of your box. Following these steps prevents unnecessary headaches. Use the router table with a small bullnose bit or a corebox bit to rout the shape.

1. Set up stop blocks to center the cut on the front edges of the lid and base, then set the fence so that half the diameter of the bit is buried in the fence.

2. Hold the lid and base (one at a time) firmly against the stop block on the left side while you lower the workpiece into the cut. Lowering the stock onto the bit prevents tearout by predrilling the area where the bit exits the wood.

WORK SMART

When routing on a nearly completed part, use a test piece to test the accuracy of the cut. Working on scrap stock gives you a chance to visualize the results without messing up the box.

CUT FINGER SLOTS IN THE LID AND BASE Rout finger slots in the front edge and lid using a corebox bit on the router table. The bit is buried in the fence so that only a portion of it engages the wood. Stop blocks control the movement of the base and lid through the cut.

Make a sliding tray

THE SLIDING TRAY IN THIS BOX IS MADE
using mitered corners with keys set in place to lock
and strengthen the joints. Gluing the bottom panel
in place locks the miters on the lower edges of the
box. Building this tray calls for the same techniques
shown in making "The Simple Lift-Lid Box," on p. 4.

**GROOVE THE TRAY
SIDES TO HOUSE THE
BOTTOM** Set the tablesaw
height to ⅛ in. and leave
⅛ in. of space between the
fence and the blade, then
groove the front, back, and
sides of the tray.

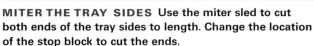

MITER THE TRAY SIDES Use the miter sled to cut
both ends of the tray sides to length. Change the location
of the stop block to cut the ends.

1. Use the miter sled to cut the mitered corners on
the four sides of the tray. Using a stop block guarantees the accuracy of matching parts (**PHOTO A**).

2. At the tablesaw, use a ⅛-in. combination blade
to cut the grooves that house the bottom of the tray
(**PHOTO B**).

3. Use the router table with a ⅛-in.-radius roundover bit to rout the upper edges of each part.

ASSEMBLE THE TRAY Tape the tray parts together
at the corners and apply glue to the miters and just a bit
in the grooves. Then roll the sides of the tray around the
bottom. Add additional tape to close the last joint, then
add tape at each corner to increase clamping pressure.

4. After sanding all the surfaces on the sides of the tray, lay the parts flat and use clear tape to hold the parts together while you spread glue in the joints and grooves. Wrap the parts around the bottom panel and apply additional layers of tape to pull the joints tight **(PHOTO C)**.

5. Use the miter-key jig on the tablesaw to cut key slots on the upper edges of each corner. As in making the simple box on p. 4, I used wider keys at the top of the box and narrower keys just below them **(PHOTO D)**.

6. Make tray supports to fit the sides of your box from ⅛-in.-thick walnut cut to the length of the inside of the box sides. Fit the supports in the grooves, but don't glue them in place yet. You'll need to remove the supports later to add or remove the interior dividers.

CUT KEY SLOTS Use the miter-key jig to cut miter-key slots on the trays. Clamp a stop block in place to control the location of the key slots.

Make the dividers

THE DIVIDERS ON THIS BOX ARE MADE using imple interlocking half-lap joints. To avoid an unsightly intersection between parts, I make one set from slightly wider stock than the other. Using the crosscut sled with a stop block clamped in place makes this work easy and accurate.

1. Cut the parts to the required length using the crosscut sled and stop block.

2. Set the blade height at one-half the width of the narrower stock and cut the half laps. Keep the stock tight against the stop block throughout the cut. If the cut is too tight, bumping the stop block very lightly following your first set of cuts can help you to get a perfect fit (**PHOTO A**).

3. Cut the parts for the tray divider next and use the same technique for fitting the half-lap joints. Because this divider is made with only a single center divider, I made it thicker to minimize wiggle and poor fit in the crosspieces. Shift the position of the stop block to widen the cut as required (**PHOTO B**).

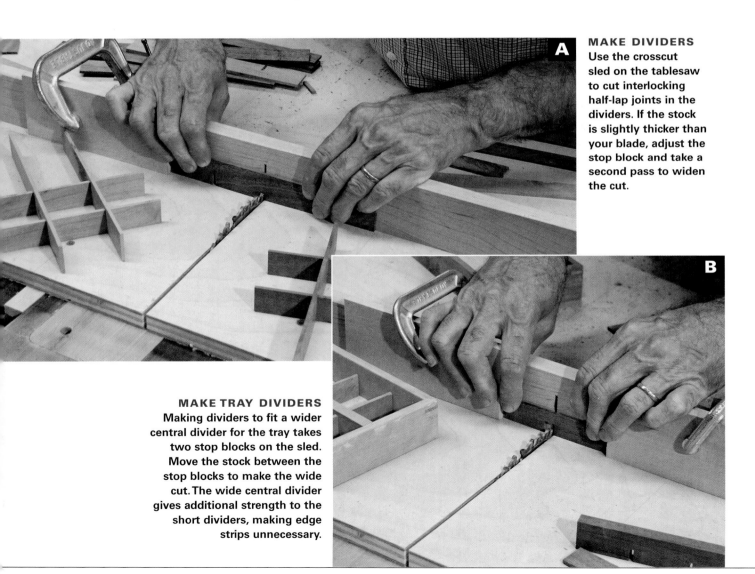

A

MAKE DIVIDERS Use the crosscut sled on the tablesaw to cut interlocking half-lap joints in the dividers. If the stock is slightly thicker than your blade, adjust the stop block and take a second pass to widen the cut.

B

MAKE TRAY DIVIDERS Making dividers to fit a wider central divider for the tray takes two stop blocks on the sled. Move the stock between the stop blocks to make the wide cut. The wide central divider gives additional strength to the short dividers, making edge strips unnecessary.

A

MAKING A STORY STICK FOR HINGES Use the table-saw and crosscut sled to nibble away a space in the story stick for the hinge to fit. You can start with careful measuring if you prefer, but this process can be done entirely by trial and error and the feel of the fit.

Ease hinge installation with a flipping story stick

INSTALLING BRASS HINGES IS THE PART OF box making that many woodworkers dread. After working on all the finer points of making a box, putting the object of your efforts at such risk can cause anxiety for even the most experienced box maker. The technique I use for cutting hinge mortises evolved over time in my shop and was inspired by the general level of frustration that hinges have always caused me. Using this method, the process is much more accurate and predictable—even fun. It all starts with what I call a "flipping story stick." Although most systems of hinge installation require careful measuring, using this system you won't even need a ruler to get accurate results.

1. Cut a piece of scrapwood on the tablesaw to the *exact* length of the box. Then make a series of cuts at the hinge location on the story stick, trimming away more and more stock until the width of the recess perfectly fits the hinge you plan to use on your box **(PHOTO A)**.

2. Check the fit of the hinge in the finished recess. A perfect fit will hold the hinge in place despite the pull of gravity. Shake the stick, however, and the hinge will fall out **(PHOTO B)**.

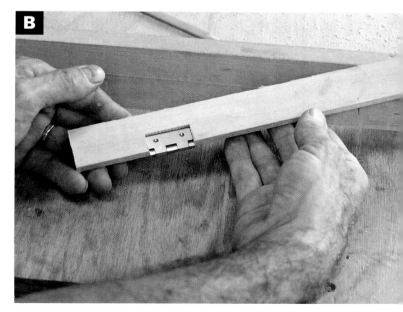

B

A PERFECT FIT A story stick with a well-fitted recess will hold the hinge securely as you slide it into place.

SET UP THE ROUTER TABLE Raise the height of the cutter so that it is just under half the thickness of the closed hinge. Take care not to rout too deep, as it causes the lid to bind at the rear of the box and not close fully at the front.

3. Place the hinge on the router table and observe carefully as you raise the height of the cutter. The height of the cutter should be just under half the thickness of the closed hinge. I use a ³⁄₁₆-in. solid carbide spiral-fluted cutter to get the best results (**PHOTO C**).

4. Use the story stick to help position the stop blocks on the router fence so that they control the movement of the lid and base. This type of hinge requires a portion of the barrel to be exposed to keep the back of the box from binding as the lid is opened. On standard butt hinges, just over half the barrel needs to be exposed, but on these hinges with a built-in stop, nearly the whole hinge barrel should be exposed at the back of the box to allow for proper movement. The position of the fence controls how much of the hinge barrel will be exposed on the back of the box. Rotate the cutter as the stop blocks are put in place. The bit needs to be at the widest point of its cut where it touches the story stick (**PHOTO D**).

SET UP THE STOP BLOCKS The story stick helps you set stop blocks to control the travel of the lid and base on the router table. For this process to be accurate, the story stick needs to be exactly the same length as the box lid and sides.

ROUT THE FIRST HINGE MORTISE
To prevent tearout, start by lowering the lid over the cutter with the lid held tightly against the left stop block. Then move the lid back and forth between the stops to form the mortise for the hinge. Make the same cuts on the base of the box.

CHECK YOUR WORK As you see here, routing leaves a round-cornered mortise, which should be squared off with a chisel before the hinges are installed.

REPOSITION THE STOP BLOCKS To locate the stop blocks for your second mortises, flip the story stick over and use it to adjust the stop blocks to their new locations. Using this method, the second mortise will be a perfectly symmetrical mirror image of the first.

5. To rout the first hinge mortise, hold the work-piece tight against the left stop block as it is lowered over the cutter. This drills the edge of the mortise rather than allowing the rotation of the cutter to tear out the back edge **(PHOTO E)**. This technique does require a little practice—it's helpful to test this technique with two pieces of scrapwood before you try it for the first time on your actual box. Rout both the lid and the base using the same setup **(PHOTO F)**.

6. This is where the flipping story stick gets its name. Flip the story stick over to guide the setup of the stop blocks you'll need to rout the matching mortises. This setup calls for exactly the same process used to cut the first mortises. The results are well-fitted hinge mortises that are perfectly symmetrical on the lid and base of the box **(PHOTOS G & H)**.

DOUBLE-CHECK THE FIT The finished hinge mortises should fit perfectly. If the fit is a bit tight, minor chiseling will work out the kinks.

Install the hinges

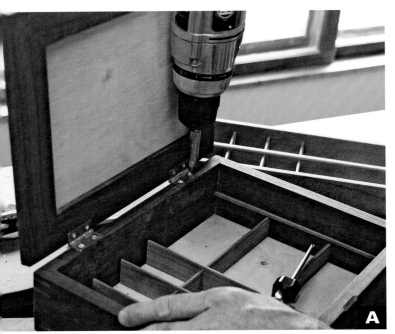

PREDRILL AND INSTALL THE SCREWS Use a vix bit to predrill holes for the brass screws. You can also do this the old-fashioned way: Use an awl to mark the center of the hole and a drill or nail sized to match the screw.

THE HINGES USED IN THIS BOX ARE BRUSSO brass hinges with a built-in 95-degree stop, making lid supports unnecessary. When installing the hinges, be sure to predrill the holes and to use beeswax to lubricate the brass screws.

1. Use a vix bit to predrill the holes for the hinges. If you don't have a vix bit, use an awl to mark the centers of the hinge holes, then predrill using a drill bit or a nail sized to fit the screws (**PHOTO A**).

2. Apply a dab of beeswax to the screw threads and use a hand-powered Phillips-head screwdriver to drive the screws into place.

Final finishing steps

THE DANISH OIL FINISH CAN BE APPLIED either before or after the hinges are mounted in place. Regardless of your choice, there are a few things to do after the box is finished and the hinges are in place. Glue the decorative lid panel in place using construction adhesive like Liquid Nails® or Leech® F-26. These adhesives work despite the presence of an oil finish and allow the decorative panel to be finished evenly on both sides prior to installation. A small bead of glue applied around the perimeter of the panel should be enough to secure it permanently in place.

The same adhesive will also work to affix the mirror inside of the lid frame. In gluing the mirror in place, take advantage of gravity to hold the mirror in place as the glue sets. Simply apply a small amount of adhesive to the back of the mirror and press it in place, then turn the box upside down while the glue sets.

As a last step, slide the dividers in place and then slip the tray support into the grooves cut on the inside surfaces of the box. None of these need to be glued in place, allowing them to be removable for easy removal of the interior dividers.

DESIGN OPTIONS

Design your box from the inside out.

DESIGNING A BOX OFTEN HAPPENS FROM THE INSIDE OUT. If I know what will go inside the finished box, I start by laying out the specific contents and making adjustments until I find a workable arrangement. For example, the arrangement of oil paints **(PHOTO A)** gives a good indication of the workable interior dimensions for an artist's box. Add enough space around the objects to allow for the wood dividers and then take measurements of the required interior dimensions. As another example, the arrangement of carving tools **(PHOTO B)** helps determine the dimensions of a carver's tool chest and determines the size of the tray inside. Simply lay the planned contents in a pleasing and effective arrangement, then use your tape measure to figure out how big your box needs to be.

MEASURE FOR A PAINT BOX Lay out the planned contents of the box and take actual measurements.

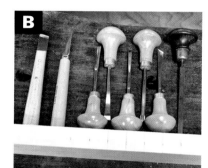

DESIGN A CARVER'S CHEST Designs are more complicated when you plan to store items that vary in size. A center divider in a simple tray is often the answer to this dilemma.

BUILD A TRAY FOR BRUSHES Organizing things is sometimes as simple as routing shallow grooves. In this tray, the grooves are sized to accommodate paint brushes.

MAKE A TOOL DIVIDER To make a tray divider for carving chisels, start by drilling a series of holes in hardwood stock. Then plane the wood until much of the waste is removed and shallow tool holders remain.

MAKING THE VARIOUS DIVIDERS or figuring out other ways to hold and organize the inside of a box can be both challenging and fun. To make a small tray divider to hold paint brushes and artist's pencils for a painter's chest, I made a series of shallow routed lines on the router table **(PHOTO C)**. To make a small holder to fit a tray on my carver's chest, I used the drill press to drill a series of holes in solid wood stock, then planed the wood down to remove most of the waste **(PHOTO D)**.

A Dovetail Box with a Wooden Hinge

BY TRADITION, DOVE-tails are associated with only the finest craftsmanship. For many, cutting dovetails by hand is a woodworker's rite of passage. Putting such egotistic notions aside, there is, in fact, a great deal of satisfaction in the quiet work of using traditional tools and techniques to gradually master a skill. From a practical standpoint, dovetails are an effective way to hold the parts of a box together and their presence is a sure sign of the time and attention of careful hands. Even if your dovetails are less than perfect, they will serve as evidence of your growth as a craftsman. On the other hand, this same box can be made beautifully and effectively using any number of joinery techniques presented earlier in this book.

The oversize wooden hinges used in this box were inspired by the work of a British box maker, Peter Lloyd, whose rustic boxes are beautiful and engaging. They are fairly simple to make using a drill press, router table, and box-joint jig.

Dovetails are a hallmark of fine work

The dovetailed box is assembled prior to adding either the lid or the base. Wooden hinges add a unique rustic charm to a simple design.

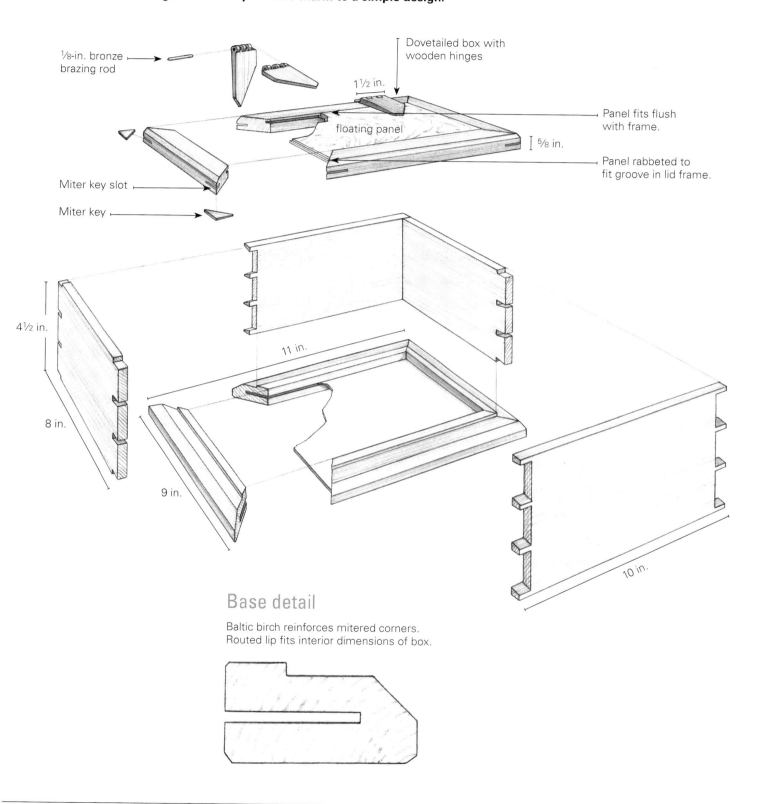

⅛-in. bronze brazing rod

Dovetailed box with wooden hinges

1½ in.

floating panel

Panel fits flush with frame.

⅝ in.

Panel rabbeted to fit groove in lid frame.

Miter key slot

Miter key

4½ in.

8 in.

11 in.

9 in.

10 in.

Base detail

Baltic birch reinforces mitered corners.
Routed lip fits interior dimensions of box.

MATERIALS

QUANTITY	PART	ACTUAL SIZE	CONSTRUCTION NOTES
2	Front and back	⅝ in. x 4½ in. x 10¹/₁₆ in.*	Walnut
2	Sides	⅝ in. x 4½ in. x 8¹/₁₆ in.*	Walnut
2	Base (front and back)	¾ in. x 1⅝ in. x 11 in.	Walnut
2	Base (sides)	¾ in. x 1⅝ in. x 9 in.	Walnut
1	Base panel	⅛ in. x 8 in. x 10 in.	Baltic birch plywood
2	Lid (front and back)	⅝ in. x 1⅜ in. x 10⅝ in.	Walnut
2	Lid (sides)	⅝ in. x 1⅜ in. x 8⁹/₁₆ in.	Walnut
1	Lid panel	⅜ in. x 6¼ in. x 8⁵/₁₆ in.	Contrasting hardwood
4	Miter keys	⅛ in. x 1¼ in. x 2½ in.	Walnut
4	Hinge leaves	⅜ in. x 1½ in. x 4½ in.	Walnut
2	Hinge pins	⅛-in. bronze rod, 2 in. long	Available at welding supply dealers

*Dimensions include ¹/₃₂-in. cleanup allowance at each end.

Cutting dovetails starts with tails

ONCE YOUR STOCK IS MILLED TO THICKNESS and cut to size, you're ready to start cutting dovetails. I use very simple tools for cutting dovetails: a marking gauge, a sliding T-bevel, a machinist square, a Japanese dozuki saw, and a few chisels. My own dovetails are never perfect, but with a bit of cleanup and an occasional sliver of thin wood to fill unwanted gaps, they result in a handsome box.

1. Set the marking gauge about ¹/₃₂ in. wider than the thickness of the stock. Hold the marking gauge tight against the end of the stock, then pull it toward you to mark both sides of each end on all four box sides (**PHOTO A**).

2. In laying out the arrangement of the dovetails, there are both practical and aesthetic considerations. The space between the dovetails needs to be wide enough for your chisels to fit. Too tight a space leads to more work and a sloppy fit. On the other hand, a wide space between the pins is a look associated with dovetails cut by router jigs. On this box and many others I make, I laid out the dovetails with ³/₁₆ in. of space between them (when measured at the outside corners). This allows a ¼-in. chisel to be used to finish the cut. Lay your dovetails out in an even pattern. I chose to do three dovetails per side, with a ¼-in.-wide half pin at the top and bottom of each side. Measure the location for your dovetails

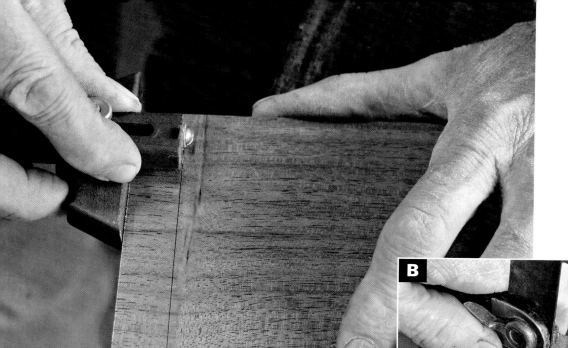

MARK THE SHAPE
OF THE TAILS Use
a sliding T-bevel set at
a 1-to-8 angle (approxi-
mately 8 degrees) to
lay out the dovetails
on the side stock.

A

SCRIBE MARKING-GAUGE LINES Begin
laying out the tails by using a marking gauge to
scribe lines on both sides of the end of each piece
of stock. The marking gauge should be set to the
thickness of the stock plus about 1/32 in. (to be
sanded away after assembly).

B

C

and then use a sliding T-bevel and pencil to mark
the tails on one of the ends. I place the tails on the
ends of the box and the pins on the front and back
(PHOTO B).

3. Transfer your markings from the first marked
end to the others. This is faster and less confusing
than measuring the tail locations on each ends of
both pieces **(PHOTO C)**.

4. Use a square and a pencil or pen to mark the
cut lines for each dovetail on the end of the stock
(PHOTO D on p. 142).

MARK THE REST OF THE PARTS Marking directly
from one set of layout lines to the adjoining part speeds
the layout process. It also helps to limit mistakes because
it guarantees that all of the tails are uniform in size and
location. Once you mark the end of the stock, use your
sliding T-bevel to mark out the tails.

MARK THE ENDS
Use a square and pencil or pen to mark the ends of the stock prior to cutting. These marks will be useful for guiding the saw in a square cut.

SAW THE TAILS Use a dozuki saw or backsaw to make the angled cuts on the tails. Watch both sides of the stock carefully and be sure that you don't cut below the marking-gauge lines.

WORK SMART

Don't let the lack of a bench vise deter you from cutting dovetails or attempting refined work. Instead of a vise, use two common wood-bodied handscrews to hold your work. Use one handscrew to hold the work-piece. Use the other handscrew to secure the first handscrew to the edge of your workbench.

5. Cut along the marked lines, stopping at the marking-gauge lines on the front and back of the stock. Begin by cutting with the saw angled in toward the marking-gauge line facing you. Then gradually change the angle of the saw until it is level and the cut reaches the marking-gauge lines on the back of the stock **(PHOTO E)**.

6. Use a chisel to remove the waste from between the sawcuts. To keep the edges of the stock crisp, your first cuts should be made slightly shy of the marking-gauge line. When the bulk of the material has been removed from between the tails, place the chisel in the line and give it a few taps to finish the cut. Chisel in from each face of the board, meeting in the middle of the stock **(PHOTO F)**.

CHISEL THE TAILS Use a narrow chisel to remove the waste from between the tails. Your first cuts should be made away from the marking-gauge line. To ensure that the last cuts are crisp and clean, set the edge of the chisel in the line created by the marking gauge.

Mark and cut the pins

1. Marking the shape of the tails onto the mating pin boards is more accurate if you use a marking knife. Clamp a piece of wood along the marking-gauge line to help hold the dovetailed stock in place **(PHOTO A)**.

2. Cut along the lines to form the pins, stopping at the marking-gauge lines on the front and back **(PHOTO B)**.

3. Use a scrollsaw or coping saw to remove the waste between the pins. This speeds your work without sacrificing the look of the hand-cut joints **(PHOTO C)**.

4. Place your chisel in the marking-gauge line and chisel down toward the center of the stock. I angle the chisel slightly greater than 90 degrees, cutting in toward the stock. Once you've chiseled to the center of the stock, flip the board over and finish chiseling from the other side **(PHOTO D)**.

MARK THE PINS The pins should be marked directly from the tails. To help with alignment, clamp a piece of scrapwood along the marking-gauge line on the inside of the dovetailed board. Use a knife to mark a crisp, accurate line.

SAW THE PINS Use a dozuki saw or backsaw to cut the lines marked out for the pins. Cut down to the marking-gauge line on both sides of the stock.

REMOVE THE WASTE Here, a scrollsaw is used to cut away some of the waste from between the pins, but a bandsaw or coping saw will work also. Take care not to cut into the pins themselves.

CHISEL THE PINS Use a wide chisel to finish removing the waste between the pins. The chisel fits neatly by feel into the marking-gauge line. Angle the chisel back toward the stock, making a slight undercut. Cut to half depth from one side, then flip the stock over to finish the cut.

Assemble the box

ASSEMBLE THE BOX Before adding any glue, be sure your clamps and clamping pads are all at hand. Spread glue on the pins and between the tails. Wiggle the parts into position and then use clamps to pull the joints tight. Small repairs can be made now or later.

BEFORE ASSEMBLING THE BOX, DRY-FIT all the dovetails, making certain there aren't any obstructions and that each corner comes together in a good fit **(PHOTO A)**. You'll also want to sand all the inside surfaces of the box sides. Once you're ready to assemble the box, be sure to have your clamps at hand before any glue is applied. To avoid leaving clamp marks on the sides of the box, have blocks of scrapwood ready to use as clamping pads. Spread a thin layer of glue on the surfaces of both the pins and the tails and then push the parts together. Use clamps to apply pressure and hold the parts together as the glue sets. As you can see in **PHOTO B**, my box had a slight miscut in the dovetails, so I glued in a sliver of walnut to strengthen the joinery. Small repairs like this will be unnoticed in the finished box.

WORK SMART

Sometimes dovetails require work that wasn't planned. If dry-fitting the joint shows a gap, cut a piece of thin stock to fill the space. If the gap is slightly misshapen, run the saw down into the gap to make it more uniform and then cut a thin piece of wood to fill the space.

Build a frame-and-panel base

THE LID AND BASE OF THIS BOX ARE MADE using a frame-and-panel technique. The base parts are mitered and assembled around a Baltic birch panel that helps reinforce the mitered joints.

1. Use a miter gauge on the tablesaw to cut the frame of the base to length. Use stop blocks to control the lengths of the parts and change the position of the stop blocks to cut each matching pair **(PHOTO A)**.

2. Cut 1⅛-in.-deep grooves on the edge of each piece. Set the fence ⅞₁₆ in. from the blade and cut with the top face against the fence.

3. Cut a piece of 1⅛-in.-thick Baltic birch plywood to fit between the grooves cut into the base frame. The plywood panel will not only act as the bottom of the box, but also help to reinforce the miter joints on the base frame.

4. Spread glue on the mitered surfaces and a bit extra into the grooves that house the bottom panel. To assemble the base, slide all the frame parts onto the bottom panel, then secure the corners with tape until the glue dries **(PHOTO B)**.

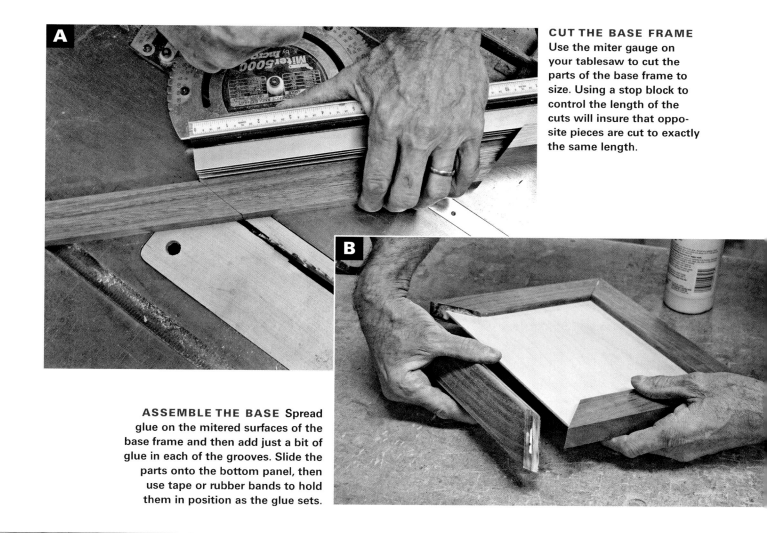

A

CUT THE BASE FRAME Use the miter gauge on your tablesaw to cut the parts of the base frame to size. Using a stop block to control the length of the cuts will insure that opposite pieces are cut to exactly the same length.

B

ASSEMBLE THE BASE Spread glue on the mitered surfaces of the base frame and then add just a bit of glue in each of the grooves. Slide the parts onto the bottom panel, then use tape or rubber bands to hold them in position as the glue sets.

ROUT A RABBET AROUND THE BASE Fit the bottom to the underside of the box by routing a rabbet along each edge. It's safer and easier to make this cut in increments rather than trying to hog it all out at once. Routing in steps also allows you to work your way to a precise fit.

5. Route a ⅛-in.-deep rabbet around the perimeter of the base to adjust its size to fit within the interior of the box sides. This will allow the box to nest over the base and be easily glued in place after finishing **(PHOTO C)**.

6. Use a chamfering bit in the router table to shape the edges of the base. After the base is sanded and finished, it will be ready to add to the finished box.

Make the lid

THE LID IS SIMILAR IN CONSTRUCTION TO the base, but because it uses solid wood as the panel material, a different method is required to secure the corners. I decided to use keyed miter joints at the corners of the lid frame, a technique used on many other boxes in this book. Rather than using a contrasting species of wood that would draw attention to the keys as a decorative element, I used walnut keys to match the walnut frame.

1. Cut and miter the frame parts of the lid, then use a ¼-in.-dado blade to groove the inside edges of each piece. This groove will house the hardwood panel set inside the frame. The saw should be set so that the blade height is ¼-in. and the distance from the fence to the outside of the blade equals the thickness of the top panel.

2. Once the panel is cut to size, you'll need to cut a tongue to fit inside the grooves on the lid frame. Set both the distance from the fence to the inside of the cut and the blade height. To make the cut, stand

FIT THE TOP PANEL To begin shaping the tongue that fits in the grooves on the lid frame, stand the top panel on edge with the bottom side flush against the fence.

the panel on end against the fence. Avoid tearout by cutting the end grain first, then the side grain **(PHOTO A)**.

FINISH FORMING THE TONGUE Make cuts into the top face of the top panel to finish forming a tongue that fits into the grooves on the lid frame. After cutting, check the actual fit of the tongue to see that it seats properly.

ASSEMBLE THE LID Use tape to hold the corners together as you apply glue to the miters. Try to avoid getting any glue in the grooves. To assemble the lid, simply roll the glued parts around the top panel.

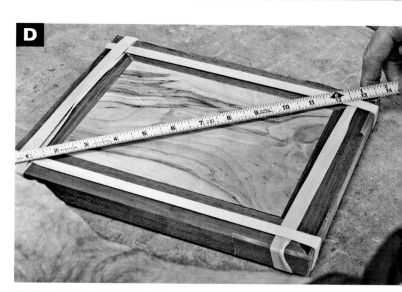

3. Adjust the blade height so that it equals the measurement from the face of the panel to the cut made in the last operation. Change the location of the fence so that the distance from the outside of the cut to the fence is ¼ in. Then finish rabbeting the panel (and forming the tongue) with the stock held flat on the saw. Again, cut the end grain first **(PHOTO B)**.

4. Apply glue to the miter joints, then assemble the frame around the panel. Use clear packing tape to hold the corners in place. In this case, where you're making a floating panel, it is best to avoid putting glue in the grooves used to house the panel. Gluing the panel in place would limit the freedom of the panel to expand and contract with seasonal changes in humidity **(PHOTO C)**.

5. Use rubber bands to pull the corners tight and double-check to see that the frame is square by measuring corner to corner from both directions **(PHOTO D)**.

CHECK FOR SQUARE Use a tape measure to check to see that your assembly is square. Each diagonal measurement should be the same. If not, hand pressure is all you need to make small adjustments.

6. Use a miter-key jig to hold the lid securely while the key slots are cut (**PHOTO E**).

7. Cut and insert miter keys in the key slots. After the glue has dried, sand the keys flush with the frame (**PHOTO F**).

8. As a final touch to the lid, use a chamfering bit in the router table to shape the edges.

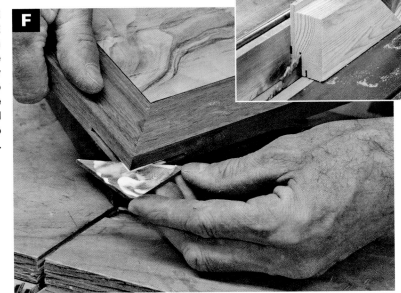

E

F

GLUE THE KEYS IN PLACE Spread glue on all surfaces of the keys, then simply slide them into place. After the glue dries, sand the keys flush to the lid frame.

CUT THE KEY SLOTS Use a miter-key jig to cut key slots in the four corners of the lid. The jig used here is the same one used on "The Simple Lift-Lid Box," on pp. 16–17. For this operation, this quick jig provides better support than the one used for larger boxes.

Install the hinges

SHOPMADE WOODEN HINGES ARE A NICE complement to the handcut dovetails on the sides of this box. Making your own wooden hinges is also a straightforward operation. For more on making wooden hinges, see "Shopmade Wooden Hinges" on pp. 150–151.

Installing wooden hinges is a fairly simple, but you'll want to make sure you don't add unnecessary stress on the hinge barrel. Because wooden hinges can be fragile when subjected to stress, they must be positioned precisely and squarely so that they can move freely throughout the normal range of motion. It helps to have a place where they nest squarely built into the design of the box. I cut mortises at the back of the lid to help position the hinges. These mortises also provide a bit of overhang at the back edge of the box.

1. Use a crosscut sled at the tablesaw to cut the recesses that will serve as mortises for the hinges. Begin by raising the blade to ¼ in. (two-thirds the thickness of one leaf of the hinge) and clamp stop blocks in place on the sled to limit the range of cuts. To cut the first mortise, make a series of passes as you move the lid between the stop blocks.

2. After cutting the first mortise, flip the lid end for end so that the opposite face of the lid is against the sled's fence. Cut the second mortise using the method in step 1 **(PHOTO A)**.

3. Test the fit to see that the hinges nest tightly into the mortises on the lid, then secure them using polyurethane glue. Though polyurethane glue is strong and up to the task of affixing these hinges, it can also be messy, so use it sparingly. As the glue cures, it will seep out from the edges of the mortise. If the glue is still wet, you can clean it up with mineral spirits. Or you can simply wait until the glue hardens, then clean it up using a sharp chisel **(PHOTO B)**.

4. Spread glue on the other half of the hinges and then clamp the hinges in place. Before clamping, I slide folded business cards between the lid and the box to provide a bit of clearance at the back of the box **(PHOTO C)**.

Finishing touches

ALL SANDING SHOULD BE DONE TO THE BOX prior to installing the hinges, but the Danish oil finish should come after the hinges are glued in place. Use construction adhesive like Leech F-26 or Liquid Nails to attach the lid to the base. Use masking tape to hold the base in position while the glue dries.

FIT THE WOODEN HINGES Mortise the lid to accept the hinge using a crosscut sled on the tablesaw and stop blocks to control the range of cuts. Setting the blade height at ¼ in. provides for a ¼-in. overhang at each edge of the finished box. To cut the second mortise, flip the stock end for end.

ATTACH THE HINGES Use polyurethane glue to attach the hinges to the lid. Watch out—too much glue can make a mess as it foams and expands when it cures. Allow the glue to set overnight before attaching the other leaf of the hinge to the body of the box.

ATTACH THE LID After the glue holding the hinges to the lid has cured, use the same gluing process to attach the hinges to the box. Having the box open at the base provides access for fitting spring clamps in place.

Although wooden hinges may not look right on every box design, they can be quite effective when you're aiming for a more rustic look. But there are challenges in making wooden hinges—particularly in making wooden hinges that last. Wooden hinges—even large ones—are more fragile than metal ones. Also, as a wooden hinge passes through a range of motion any inaccuracies in the way it is machined can cause stresses that lead to failure. When that failure takes place on your highly crafted box, it can be most disappointing. For that reason, I prefer to think of my wooden-hinged boxes as recreational and experimental. If they last a few years to remind me of the fun I had making them, I consider them a success.

Making a wooden hinge requires careful setup of your tools. I use a drill press outfitted with a fence to position the holes drilled in the barrel of the hinge. I also use a broken-off and resharpened ⅛-in. drill bit to drill the holes for the hinge pin. The reason I use a broken off bit is because longer bits often bend and wander as you drill. Shortening the drill bit lessens the amount of flex in the bit.

1. Set the fence on your drill press to drill through the center of your hinge stock. I use a dial caliper to check the measurements on both sides of a test hole. When you're satisfied that the hole is centered in the test stock, use it as a guide to set the stop block that positions the hole from the end of the hinge stock. I simply lower the drill into the hole and slide the stop block in place **(PHOTO A)**.

2. Drill in from one side to just past the midpoint in the depth of the stock, then flip the stock over with the opposite face against the fence and drill until you feel the drill enter the hole from the other side. Some amount of overlap in the depth from both sides is helpful in preventing the hinge pin from binding in the operation of the hinge **(PHOTO B)**.

SET THE STOP BLOCK After setting the fence to drill the center of the hinge stock, use your test piece to position the stop block. The drill should fit an equal distance from each side and the end.

CUT THE KNUCKLES Use a box-joint jig to cut the interlocking fingers on the leaves of the hinge. I use a ¼-in. dado blade and a ¼-in. drill bit as a guide pin.

3. Use a roundover bit in the router table to shape the barrel of the hinge parts. To help direct the workpiece across the bit safely, hold the stock tightly against a backing board **(PHOTO C)**.

4. Use a box-joint jig on the tablesaw to cut simple box joints in each piece **(PHOTO D)**. For more details on the jig and cutting box joints, refer to pp. 42–43.

DRILL FOR THE HINGE PINS With the drill press set to drill to just over half the depth of the stock, drill in from one edge, then turn the stock over to drill from the opposite side.

SHAPE THE BARREL Use a ³⁄₁₆-in. roundover bit in the router table to shape the barrels of the hinges. Using a guide board holds the hinge leaves square to the fence when the edge no longer contacts the guide bearing on the router bit.

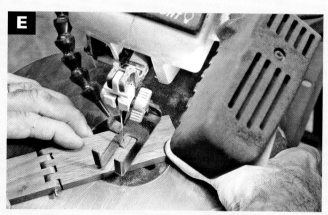

CUT THE HINGES TO SHAPE Use a scrollsaw to cut the hinges to shape. The scrollsaw cuts don't need to be perfect because you'll clean up the edges by sanding.

TAPER AND SMOOTH THE HINGES Use the belt sander to shape the hinges. The hinges are tapered toward the ends and a slight bevel softens the edges.

5. Fit the fingers of both hinge leaves into each other and then tap ⅛-in. bronze or brass welding rod into place as your hinge pin.

6. Once the hinge pin is installed you can cut the hinge leaves to whatever shape pleases you. I chose an angular look consistent with the shape of the dovetails and mitered corners used in this box **(PHOTO E)**.

7. I give additional interest and shape to my hinges by using the stationary belt sander. Thin the leaves toward the end to give the hinge a more delicate look **(PHOTO F)**.

DESIGN OPTIONS

This simple dovetailed box presents numerous options for altering the design. By replacing the wooden hinges with more conventional hardware, the design becomes classic and formal. By replacing the panel top with a single wide piece of spalted maple with a natural edge and a small protrusion forming a finger pull, the box fitted with sculpted hinges becomes an even wilder investigation in the world of rustic work.

A CLASSIC DESIGN To install the brass hinges, I used a technique borrowed from the chapter on making a jewelry box with a sliding tray. For more on this process, see the box on p. 118. Because the lid is wider than the base in this box, I used two story sticks, one for the lid and one for the base. I set the fence on the router table a greater distance from the cutter to create a blind mortise in the lid. I also moved the fence in toward the cutter to cut the mortises for the base of the box so that the barrel of the hinge would protrude and provide clearance for the box to open.

1. Use a story stick to position the stop blocks on the router table. The story stick must be the exact length of the part of the box being mortised (**PHOTO A**).

2. Predrill the holes for mounting the hinges and lubricate the screws to keep them from shearing off in the wood.

3. Add a lid support to control the movement of the lid. This type of support works well with the standard brass butt hinges used in making this box (**PHOTO B**).

SET UP FOR BRASS HINGES Use story sticks (as described on p. 133) to set up the router table and stop blocks to rout mortises for the hinges. This box requires a total of four stop-block setups to accommodate the overlapping lid.

ADD THE LID SUPPORT Another advantage of making a box with a removable base is that it provides access for installing lid supports. Installing hardware like this without being able to see its exact placement requires extensive trial and error.

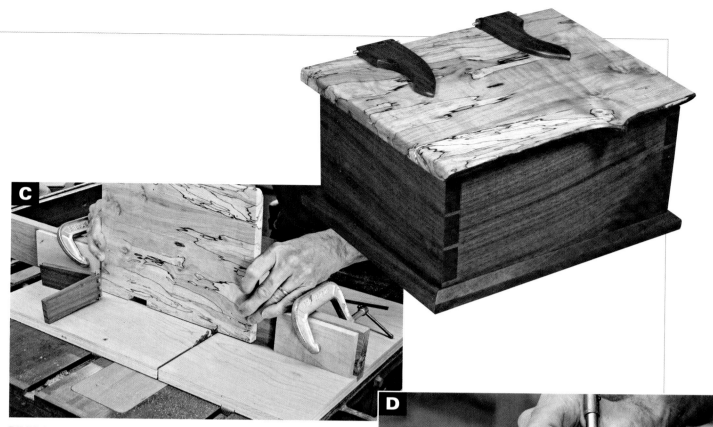

PREPARE LID FOR HINGE INSTALLATION Use the tablesaw to cut hinge mortises in the back of the lid. The space between stop blocks allows you to cut mortises by making a series of cuts with a single blade.

DESIGN THE HINGES Design your hinges by placing them on your box and sketching in pen or pencil. I used hinges from an earlier box for inspiration. Use your imagination and engage in play. Using a pencil will allow you to erase designs until you come up with one you like.

A RUSTIC BOX WITH A PANEL LID To make an even more rustic box, cut a solid panel to size and use it for the lid of the box. Then shape the leaves of the hinges in an even more sculptural pattern.

1. Cut hinge mortises at the back of the solid wood lid using the tablesaw cutoff sled and the blade raised to ⅜ in. Use stop blocks to control the range of the cuts as you move the workpiece between stops. After cutting the first mortise, flip the lid so that its opposite face is against the sled and cut a mortise on the other side of the lid **(PHOTO C)**.

2. Design your hinges with a pen or pencil. Designs evolve through time and study of past work. For the box shown here I used a box crafted earlier as inspiration for designing new hinges. Cut the hinges to shape using a scrollsaw and then sand them to more delicate proportions using a stationary belt sander **(PHOTO D)**.